To Bub
I enjoy your friendship,
Hope you
enjoy
the Road

Howard

Coast to Coast

with

A Cat

and

A Ghost

Judy Howard

ISBN: 1461153786
ISBN-13: 9781461153788
LCCN: 2011907228

Praises for
Coast To Coast With A Cat And A Ghost

Preface

The chemo and radiation months passed with raw emotion bandaged tightly. He remained the strongest man I ever knew and I continued to do what I thought was impossible, I dealt with it. We were both struggling souls trying to fit into a world we didn't always understand. I had grown strong over the years fighting his will to control and dominate. He grew loving and tender as he tempered his fears and angers. We needed each other's weaknesses to grow. I had grown strong enough to let go and he had grown strong enough in his love to soar to the heavens.

I couldn't help him on his last journey but I lay beside him, breathing in his spirit for the last time. He passed, soaring peacefully to some unknown realm. His last breath seemed like my last too. It was as if a knife had just sliced us apart. But just past the piercing pain, it became like a clear day to me and I could see forever as I began to understand everything. Our difficulties had molded us and shaped us into this entity that would always be one even in goodbye.

When her husband of 25 years passes away, Judy Howard is faced with confusing feelings and an overwhelming sense of loss. Accompanied by her cat, Sportster, and a stuffed doll whose uncanny and somewhat unsettling resemblance to her late husband leads to her calling it Jack Incarnate, Howard takes to the road on an RV trip from her home on California's Pacific coast to Florida's Atlantic. And what happens next surprises even her.

A touching, poignant, and empowering journey of discovery—and self-discovery, Howard's debut is an inspiring road story full of surprises and universal truths. Beginning with a sobering and altogether real accounting of death, the author quickly regains her footing and seizes her life with courage and gusto. The antics of Sportster in addition to Jack Incarnate's needling comments add lightness and humor while she experiences the challenges and fears and yet wonderful discoveries of a road trip. From the fear and unsettling circumstance of leaving everything familiar behind to the challenge of crossing Lake Pontchartrain to dealing with the spirit of Jack and seeing, for the first time, the Atlantic Ocean, this middle-aged bildungsroman clarifies for Howard her life's path, and in the end, she comes to terms with her deep love for Jack despite the abuse that was a part of their relationship, emerging a stronger woman for it.

Weaving an emotionally charged narrative with humorous anecdotes and a unique perspective on life, Howard's odyssey of overcoming grief to find her true self is, in essence, the story of each of us. Full of heart and a budding fearlessness, this quintessential road trip delivers on every level, as moving and fulfilling as it is entertaining. Powerfully written and eloquently understated, *Coast to Coast with a Cat and a Ghost* is the most surprising and satisfying memoir in recent memory.

Coast to Coast

with

A Cat

and

A Ghost

Judy Howard

Acknowledgements

I am indebted to so many who have traveled with me on this amazing journey, changing my worn out words and pointing out the detours.

First, I want to thank each and every of the many chance encounters whose names I never even knew; the many to whom I told my stories. Although you told me I was your inspiration, you all in turn, have enlightened me in a wonderful way I could never have imagined. Thank you all.

Secondly, Denver Howard. With humility and unawareness of your creative talents, you spit out the title as if it were an afterthought. It is your creative genius, Denver that has made this book complete with its "haunting" title, that it may lure the reader into a realm of magical adventure. Thank you Denver.

To my dearest Sandy. Your honesty and attention to detail sprinkled generously with your sisterly love and encouragement has carried me through the "rough blocks", the "bad neighborhoods", the dirt roads my mind has taken me. You may rest knowing that you have given me and, consequently, many others the opportunity to travel on a magical journey of discovery.

Thanks to "new" Vickie (Vickie Delaney) and "old" Vickie (Vickie Andreotti), Archie and John Wymer, Clarice Diorio, and so many others who have invested their editing skills and honest opinions to keep me on the right road. I will always be indebted.

And finally, the most serendipitous event in this journey, thank you to all the members of my writing group in Hemet, Ca. Ann Dunham and Susan Squier, Gila Shabanow, Norma Garwood, Richard Wyatt, Bill Fleming -- all of you have been the polishers, the tinkerers, the finishers, the detailers who have made me shine. You will always be in my heart.

Therefore, with all said and done, it also takes a village to write a book. I hope everyone has a magical adventure reading, **Coast To Coast With A Cat And A Ghost.**

Yours truly,
Judy Howard (and Sportster)

THIS BOOK IS DEDICATED TO "MY GHOST" AND MY 'BESTEST' FRIEND, JACK LEDGER HOWARD. MAY YOUR SPIRIT SOAR AS HIGH AS YOU HAVE LIFTED MINE. THANK YOU FOR THE GOOD AND THE SEEMINGLY BAD. YOUR SPIRIT WILL FOREVER LIVE THROUGH ME.

Chapter One

The miles drifted past my windshield as the rumbling sound of the engine played background to the radio's soft country twang. I was lulled into a spiritual state as the sounds lured me down forgotten memory lanes. The motor home steadily ate up the warm, black asphalt as I traveled on this long-anticipated journey. My mind hesitantly took one of those exits on memory lane and I drifted to a long, hot summer day when I was forced to say good-bye to my beloved husband, Jack. His time on this earth was nearly over, but he wanted to go out with his boots on, so determined he was not to be weak. He broke my tortured heart as he struggled to rise, trying to overcome his weakness. Frustrated, he spoke my name like a mantra, hoping I could help. I cried inside.

I had never cried in front of him since the day he was diagnosed. That day we were both raw with fear and stripped of hope and he, hot with anger. Jack lashed and lunged at the cancer's grip that limited his time and the air that he breathed, and I was in the way. I sobbed at his attack, knowing his emotional wounds had to be excruciating. Tears flooded my face and poured into his heart. His heart, already full of his pain, could not handle mine too. As he begged me not to cry, he wrapped his arms, that would always be strong for me and cradled me for one last time.

From that day forward, I cried alone. I lost my best friend that day. The loneliness seared my brain and stopped my heart. Jack had a battle to fight. He had no time for my fears, my hurts. I was on my own. Not until that day did I realize that the bond of togetherness, partnership, and devotion, which I had foolishly ignored, was now lost forever. How could I go on? How could I possibly hold it together? How could I let him go? How would I tell him it was okay to go? Oh God, how could I do this?

The chemo and radiation months passed, with our emotions still raw but bandaged tightly. He remained the strongest man I ever knew, and I continued to do what I thought was impossible: I dealt with it. We were both struggling souls trying to fit into a world we didn't always understand. I had grown strong over the years by fighting his will to control and dominate. He grew loving and tender as he tempered his fears and angers. We needed each other's weaknesses if we were to grow. I had grown strong enough to let go, and he had grown strong enough in his love to soar to the heavens.

I couldn't help him on his last journey, but I lay beside him, breathing in his spirit for the last time.

He passed, soaring peacefully to some unknown realm. His last breath seemed like my last too. It was as if a knife had just sliced us apart. But just past the piercing pain, it became like a clear day to me, and I could see forever as I began to understand everything. Our difficulties had molded us and shaped us into this entity that would always be one, even in good-bye.

It had been only four months since that hot August afternoon when I had to say good-bye to my best friend of twenty-five years. Jack had come onto this earth with the fireworks on the Fourth of July and now, as a rare summer thunderstorm performed a grand finale for his exit, he began his new journey, free of pain. And so my lonely pain and widowhood began.

He was done now and so was I. He wasn't coming back. I grabbed the walker that parked now, unneeded, at the foot of the bed. I ran down the hall to the garage and hurled it into the empty space where his Harley had been. It landed with a loud metal clamor that was not loud enough. I grabbed an empty box from the garage and stormed back into the house. I yanked open the medicine-cabinet door. I shoved countless prescription bottles off their shelves and clattering into the box. Still not loud enough. I dragged every last piece of medical equipment, screeching, across the tiled floor, and tossed each one the walker -the nebulizer –the beside urinal into the pile in the garage. It was all dead to me. Everything lay scattered on the garage floor in the empty space where his beloved Harley had been parked.

I wanted to see no more illness. I wanted to take a sledgehammer to all the hateful reminders. I wanted to be done with it. I just wanted to remember him, to remember us, before the monster had sprung on us. I wanted to go back to the joking, teasing times, the quiet oneness times.

During those darkest days of his illness, a seed was sown in my imagination of a better place, a place to escape the pain and sorrow. I began to travel in my mind. First it was a local camping trip, sitting in the shade of a California oak while inhaling the sweet scent of lush green grass, with a warm spring breeze whispering in my ear. As I endured those never-ending, agonizing days of grief, the seed began to sprout. The California oak became an Arizona saguaro and then a Florida cypress dripping with Spanish moss. My imagination took me roaming across the country, where I was humbled by majestic vistas and felt the reverence of historic landmarks. The seed pushed its way up through those hopeless days as Jack traveled his own lonely road, bringing him closer and closer to his journey's end, and me to my journey's beginning.

The dream that I had nurtured safely in the confines of illness and responsibilities now began to take command. The vision of driving across this great country after he was gone, experiencing its history and feeling the heartbeat of its people, was always in my mind's sight. Even in sleep, the vision would appear, unwilling to be ignored. But dreams don't just spring into reality like the pop-up on a child's birthday card; they take planning and a lot of courage. I knew how to plan, but where would I get courage? The Wizard of Oz was no-where in sight.

My courage came disguised as a Winnebago that we had purchased a few years before Jack's illness. Twenty-four feet was considered small in RV circles, but to me was long enough. Winnebago made several models. Eerily, the one we had chosen was called "Spirit." Sweeping lines of purples and blues graced the white, wide body outside, and a large Harley Davidson sticker on the rear window announced the partiality of a now–ghost rider. Two beefy wheels in front and dualies, as they are called, in the rear carried this home that would be the bravado for my courage, my wom-an cave. When I drove this big rig, I grew several inches and became buff. I was now the shadowy image who looked down from the darkened cab into your car's passenger window. I was the envy of all who dreamt my dream. The hugeness of the motorhome's appearance to the outside world ended when you entered. All the comforts of home existed in scaled-down versions. A tiny kitch-en with a tinier sink, microwave, stove, oven, and refrigerator, was just big enough to be adequate. The limited space in the bathroom had a shower that was big enough to stand in but difficult to move around in. And the toilet was the right size to start the job, but limited space made it awk-ward to finish. The snug bed framed by large win-dows gave a hundred-and-eighty-degree view of the nighttime starlight shows. And finally the living room, decorated in mauves and mochas, allowed me to either enjoy the scenic view out the tinted picture window, or relax to my favorite TV show or movie on the high-def flat screen. Life could be very good on the road.

Any journey begins with one step. For me it was one mile. The cushioned armrests wrapped around me as I sank into the driver's seat. With sweaty hands and a thumping pulse, I felt every inch and pound of fiberglass and metal weighing on my shoulders. My shaky foot stepped on the gas and slowly, very slowly, I crept away from the curb, heading for practice destinations of nearby campgrounds that Jack and I had frequented. With heavy heart and fond memories at each campground, I sprinkled Jack's ashes at our favorite spots. I remembered the good times and the bad times, and cried. Then I would vow my love to him, falling down on my knees and begging God to somehow give me just one more day with him. I became more and more comfortable with driving, backing in, hooking up, and unhooking (very important too). And I became more familiar with my new painful passenger called loneliness.

Necessity was the mother of invention, and that was how Jack became reincarnated. Watching the movie *Cast Away*, with Tom Hanks, I had become inspired by his relationship with the volleyball, "Wilson." Out of desperation and loneliness, I too created a companion. Sewing feverishly and stuffing a cloth body, arms, and legs; gluing plastic eyes and hanks of wig hair, I created a life-sized doll that looked amazingly real.

Jack was a Harley man to the core. If you did not own a Harley or at least lust for one, you were not of much interest to him. Jack's reincarnation began with Harley boots on the feet, while the fabric head sprouted just enough hair for a ponytail secured by a rawhide tie. A Harley earring dangled from the correct ear, and, of course, a Harley T-shirt, announcing "Harley Rules," fit snuggly over his polyester chest. Topping his bald head was, of course, a Harley hat, while dark glasses shaded the glued-on buggy blue eyes. A gaudy ring and an imitation gold–encrusted watch wrapped his finger and wrist. I was now no longer alone: Jack Incarnated was riding shotgun.

Although I was never a cat lover, a cat indeed became the next addition to my traveling family. Sportster arrived at my doorstep looking for a home. Moved by the belief that if an animal was born after the death of a loved one, a piece of that loved one's soul could be transferred into the newborn's soul, I took him in.

Wanting to be a responsible pet owner, I needed to establish Sportster's birth date for future celebrations. The vet determined the little guy to be six weeks old. I got chills when I discovered that, counting back exactly six weeks from his arrival date, his birthday was my birthday! Any doubts I had about keeping the cat vanished. Had I known that this little spirit was born that day, with his destiny to enhance my stark life, I would not have wept on my first birthday alone. I would have rejoiced instead. I was now a cat lover.

Was part of Jack reincarnated into this little soul? Jack had always been uncomfortable with displays of affection. Although I knew he welcomed my kisses, he would always pooh-pooh them with a cavalier attitude. Sportster sat on the high back of my recliner as I brought my face near to kiss his small pink nose. The nearer my lips became to his nose, the further his head leaned back until, losing his balance, he fell to the floor, albeit gracefully.

Life with Jack had been orderly and clean. When he had a painting chore, the paint was applied only to the intended surfaces. It never ended up on him or his clothes, a feat I found impossible. When I was painting the closet one day, Sportster found his way into my work space. I was covered in paint, and dared not grab him or he would also be covered from paw to tail. I was forced to allow him to wander through the closet. He inspected my job and meandered out again without a speck of paint touching his pristine fur. I was now a believer in this phenomenon of reincarnation, since this feline had graced my life without my invitation, never making a mess and allowing me to admire him only at a distance. So Sportster was now on board too, along with Jack Incarnate, both ready for the adventures ahead. Sportster was perched unconcerned on the dash, Jack Incarnate had his wide-eyed navigator's stare, and I watched the landscape drift by. My home and friends, along with the miles, were disappearing in the rearview mirror. There were no holds on me now, no one to answer to; I was running wild and free.

I was running away from home just like I had when I was eight.

"Can we sleep out in the tent tonight?"

"No, it's going to rain."

My father's deep voice, and my and my sister's light musical chatter, echoed in the halls of my memory. My sister, Sandy and I looked at each other with disappointed but mischievous eyes and decided simultaneously that we would be denied nothing; besides, Dad was no weatherman. Sis headed for the attic, sneaking the necessary blankets, pillows, and bags of potato chips. I slipped outside, and rounded up our LaBrentor retriever that Dad had trained, when we were toddlers, to pull us in a cart. I hooked up the dog, who was tolerant of our childish whims, and led him around to the side of the house, stopping under the second-story attic window. I peered up into a crisp blue sky with puffy white clouds and no rain in sight. From the attic window, Sis was lowering tied bundles of blankets and pillows down to me on a rope, and I efficiently packed everything. Sis then scrambled downstairs and out the back door, probably slamming the screen door in her excitement. She joined me and we headed out. We were running away from home, doing what we wanted, with no one telling us what to do. We were on our own.

Crossing the street and cutting through the neighbors' yards, we headed for the acres of open farmland. We traveled what we were sure was one hundred child miles, then stopped to settle our camp in a small grove of trees beside a cornfield. The flat land barely allowed us to see our house across the vast cornfield as dusk began to creep into the grove. I unhooked our loyal LaBrentor from the cart as Sis carefully laid out the blankets, placing the pillows side by side. We sat on the blanket, munched our chips, and began to think of home. As our thoughts went to Mom and Dad, guilt began to steal its way into camp, masking itself as cool evening shadows. We didn't want Mom and Dad to worry about us, putting our pictures on milk cartons and crying into the night that they should not have treated us so badly. So it was decided that Sis would return home to inform them that we were, in fact, running away from home and that we were just fine. She trekked off into the evening shadows. As I sat with my arm tightly around the dog, waiting for her return, I listened to the soft clicking of crickets and the whispering omens of an owl.It began to rain. It didn't seem long before Sis covered those one hundred child-miles home and back again to camp. The rain was coming down steadily, and darkness had stolen into camp without my noticing until now.

"They said we have to come home."

I don't think we said anything more to each other as we packed our things back into the cart, hooked up the poor wet dog, and headed home. That was the day we ran away from home.

But now, half a lifetime later, I really was running away from home. I would be leaving my life as I knew it. Sun City had been my home for over twenty years. I knew the cars on the streets, and who were in the cars that drove on the streets. I knew the owner of the local repair garage by his first name, and the bank tellers and grocery clerks knew mine. I had lovingly cared for my home, painting it, repairing its small aches and pains, shining its countertops, shampooing its carpet, and trimming and feeding its plants. It stood sturdy with self-esteem, ready to shelter me from the rains and winds of time.

I would be leaving my dog grooming business that had supported me for many years, and the customers human and furry alike who brought it life. It breathed easily under my employees' care. Helen, my manager had swept into town with a flourish a couple of years ago from the Midwestern state of Ohio and hadn't stopped moving yet. Her workaholic personality made her a perfect manager as she climbed the hairy ladder from dog bather to groomer and manager in less than a year. The other two girls, Kelly and Sheri were warm and caring with the clients as well as their owners. They were both young and full of love and life with the entire world in front of them. Kelly was a newly wed at the age of twenty and she and her new husband lived in a small mobile home taking care of her ninety –three year old grandfather. Sheri had already been trained as a groomer and had enough experience to handle unexpected occruences if they arose. She too was married and the religious sort, quiet and almost shy. It may have hiccupped a little as I left town, but it would rally to the occasion of being on its own until I returned.

My friends and my employees (who were also my friends) were my support group, the ones to whom I reported my daily comings and goings and the everyday details in between. As I left I knew that their thoughts and good wishes would ride with me, but I would miss the touch of their warm hugs and their musical bantering.

The preparation and planning was now done. The Wizard of Winnebago was gassed up, with oil changed and new tires and belts. I almost could see it doing a anxious, eager prance as it waited for me to fire up its engine I had made many lists, packed, and finally checked off the last list. My entire walk-in closet was shoved into the tiny RV closet. I was sure that as soon as I opened the closet doors again, the compacted contents would ooze out of theirprisonlike compartment and shove me to the floor. The miniature RV freezer was full of small, one-meal squares of Tupperware stacked like building blocks. Jack Incarnate was dressed in his Harley best, and, with a click of the seat belt, he was secured in the passenger seat, patiently waiting for the adventure to begin. Sportster was crouched and watched closely but not too closely, maintaining a cat's proper degree of barely disguised apathy.

All that was left to do now was question my sanity. What if something went wrong? What if I broke down? What if I got lost? How many miles would I drive a day? I had to do all the worrying, all the thinking about every detail and all the things that could go wrong. The worrying had always been Jack's job in our relationship.

The worrying was no fun, no fun at all. I laid awake nights driving the miles in my mind. The last days at home, I wanted to cry, I wanted to scream, I just wanted to go. And then the day came. The postponement of preparation could not be dragged out any longer. It was time to head out with the Wizard of Winnebago, Jack Incarnate, and Sportster the cat.

At daybreak, with excitement subdued by worries, I climbed into the driver's seat, braced myself, and took a long deep breath. I memorized my home, and my neighbors' homes, and soaked up the essence of the community. I was going to miss the stability, the quiet, and the security of my life here, but it was time to go if I were going to make it to Vickie's house for Thanksgiving. I let out that deep breath that I'd been holding for months. I turned the ignition and with a snort and I swear a stomping of its rubber tires I could feel its 'muscles' quiver in excitement.I stepped on the accelerator and, in what seemed like five minutes, loaded with every possible comfort from home, the wheels began to roll away from the curb.

My Wizard of Winnebago pranced past the city limit sign and approached the on-ramp, the gateway to the land of Oz. Easing onto the interstate, back straight, grip firm, I settled into the slow lane, checking side mirrors, gauges, and road signs while Sportster slept on the dash. Watching him sleep twisted my heart because he was totally unconcerned about the road ahead and not aware that his simple little life was held in my sweaty palms. His complete serenity reminded me to unwind the tenseness in my shoulders and watch the world that was passing by my windshield.

The exits and street signs became less familiar as the miles and minutes began to mount. Already I was drawn to signs inviting me to visit a historic landmark or to eat delicious home-cooked food. The sun was rising over the distant hills in a faraway land in front of me. The asphalt was a black river that flowed into the hills and disappeared. My anticipation grew as this first day got used up and turned into miles from home.

Chapter Two

Life on the road was a long series of beautiful paintings scrolling by the window, interrupted only by pauses at rest stops and gas stations. In cruise control, I became used to the purring of the engine, the whooshing of the passing cars, the click-click of the tires crossing asphalt cracks, and the rattle, knock-knock of the curtains and the cupboard items that made a rhythm to the traveling motion. The hours passed, and the sounds soothed me into enjoying the desert panorama as the morning sun moved across the crisp blue sky. Suddenly, *whoosh*! A trucker eased past, his air draft nudging against me, disturbing my reverie. Soon a road sign announced:

Rest Area 2 miles

It was time to pull in and stretch my legs.

Trucks and RVs →

I slipped into the diagonal parking, The Wizard dwarfed by two big semis on either side. A trucker was walking beside his rig with a tire iron and whacking his tires. Various groups of travelers were standing by their cars, visiting, or waiting for other members of their group to return from the restrooms. Other travelers watched their youngsters run off miles of stored-up energy, while still others were dutifully tending to their dogs' needs in the pet area.

I glanced over at Jack Incarnate, who shook his head, indicating he needed neither a restroom break nor to stretch his polyester-stuffed legs. Sportster raised his head from his sleep position on the dash and asked, Why we are stopped? I patted his sleepy head, climbed down from the cab while consciously checking the keys in my hand, and locked the door.

Nodding to the trucker with the tire iron, I wandered over to the patio area, where I studied a big display case with a large map, under glass that listed points of interest, mileage from here to there, and information about indigenous plants and wildlife. After a brisk ten-minute walk around the area I headed back to The Wizard of Winnebago. Inside, I was comforted by the fact that I had my own bathroom, with no waiting, unlike at the filthy public restrooms at many rest stops. I grabbed a diet Pepsi from the fridge, double-checked my maps, and Jack Incarnate again stated that he needed nothing and was just enjoying the travelers as they passed by outside, smiling and pointing at him. Sportster had been aroused from his co-navigator's seat, and demanded a treat. We were all refreshed and ready to head out again.

Making sure the refrigerator and cabinet doors were secure, I eased into the driver's seat and turned on the ignition. Satisfied with the engine's purr, I checked traffic, pulled out, and accelerated as I merged onto the interstate.

Next stop, fuel. But first, another hundred miles or so, with more rhythmic whooshing, click-clicking, rattling, and knock-knocking. The gentle, calming sounds created a perfect balance to the tense alertness that driving requires, allowing my mind to stroll and wander, to plot and plan, to remember and dream. I was alone with my roaming thoughts, hundreds of strange miles from home,but wrapped warmly in blankets of rhythmic noise and surrounded by familiar pillows and favorite foods. This phenomenon was truly unique and I became accustomed to this homey, homeless feeling.

Truck stops were always the best place to gas up, with plenty of room to pull through, turn around, or park. Big rigs rumbled in and out, just like at the rest stops. Massive motor homes towing tiny toy-looking cars took up forty to fifty feet at the pump. And inside awaited a shopping experience that would steal valuable travel time. For the tired truckers, there were restrooms and hot showers, with towels provided. Along with regular snacks and drinks there was an array of electronics, DVDs, CBs, MP3s, and GPSs. There wereT-shirts, coats, sandals, boots, and hats. Jewelry, books, plants, and of course the usual postcards and souvenirs filled the shelves.. The weary, hungry traveler was confronted by this marvel of merchandise as he entered the truck-stop restaurant, famous for "good home cookin'." This old restaurant still had the dial-up phones along with the table-sized juke-boxes at each booth, allowing the lonely trucker to call home or listen to his favorite top-ten country hits while he enjoyed country-fried steak and mashed potatoes.

I avoided all the commotion and commodities inside the truck stop by paying at the pump. After filling up, I pulled away and found a place to park. Again I asked Jack Incarnate what he needed; again, he needed nothing. What a traveler! Sportster had risen from some cubbyhole to inspect our progress, and insisted on a drink of water from the faucet. He always insisted on fresh water, training me early on to adjust the faucet to a fast drip for his drinking pleasure. Now we both decided a snack was in order. I put together a sandwich while I relaxed at the table and watched the heartbeat of the truck stop. Hissing air brakes and droning diesel engines mixed together with children's chatter as they ran from their captive cars into the respite of the restaurant. Some travelers stood near the restaurant door and away from the pump activity to smoke a cigarette or talk on their cell phones. A couple of long-legged bikers leaned against their Harleys, sipping cold beers. My heart twisted sharply in remembrance of my own Harley guy. Finishing up my sandwich to the sound of crunching cat food, I poured another Pepsi and went through what would become a routine of checking doors and, always, the cat's position, to make sure he was still on board. Tummies full, shoulders unwound, fingers uncramped, we headed out again.

The day's end was nearing as I pulled into a little town with a big reputation: Quartzite, Arizona. It was ten miles past the Arizona state line, halfway between Los Angeles and Phoenix, and was in the middle of nowhere. This little town barely supported a population of one thousand residents all year long. Until January.

An unusual phenomenon occurred in the desert in January. Aerial photographs had been taken of this little town and the surrounding desert in July. True to the little town's reputation, the photos demonstrated clearly that there was indeed nothing but cactus dotting the landscape for miles, but in January, another aerial photo showed the same cactus-dotted landscape now sprouting thousands, close to a million, white dots of RV rooftops. Every year in January, RVs from everywhere migrated to this little town that hosted what has been crowned "The World's Largest Swap Meet," causing the local population to explode to a nation of one million. While the surrounding desert was dotted with white RV rooftops, the five square miles within the town's limits was also spotted with a multitude of multicolored tent tops. These tents shaded thousands of tables, full of wares of whatever sort the mind could imagine, from the heat of the desert sun.

One huge circus-sized tent sold everything and anything that the RV'er could possibly need, and whatever the hawker could convince him that he needed. There were hundreds of other individual small tents, tables, and booths. They had a myriad of goods being peddled by herds of nomads who traveled from craft fairs to state fairs to street fairs, setting up their booths and, when the gig was over, packing it in and moving on to the next venue. They were a fascinating crowd, these people of the road, as well as the flocks who bought their wares. Combined in this spectacle were also an RV show, antique car show, rock and mineral show, an arts and crafts show, and a bluegrass festival.

Quartzite's original name was Tyson Wells; it was a way station for the stage that carried military and mining supplies from Eherenberg to Prescott in the 1850s. The town boasted The Hi Jolly Cemetery and Monument that was named after Philip Tedro. He was a Greek born in Syria and, after making a pilgrimage to Mecca, changed his name to Hadji Ali and immigrated to America. He was hired as a camel driver by the cavalry in an experiment to use camels to transport supplies across the Arizona desert. After the experiment failed, Hadj Ali remained in the area as a scout, prospector, and courier for what was called Jackass Mail. Unable to pronounce his Islamic name, locals called him "Hi Jolly." After his death, a monument had been built, and still remained. It was the highlight in the town's little cemetery that now was home to many pioneers of what was now named Quartzite, Arizona. Like many others, Jack and I made this pilgrimage every year. We always visited the Hi-Jolly Cemetery. While the surrounding hills and mountains enfolded the little town, offering a striking view, the words on the tombstones carried us back in time.

So this tiny town, with a strange and colorful past, remained strange and colorful. It attracted every economic class. Dry-docked in the desert, monstrous million-dollar motor homes towing Hummers would be parked next to a homemade camper held together by baling wire, the living quarters of an unfortunate soul who had not bathed in weeks and was just trying to sell his meaningless items for cash to buy gas. And there were the regular folk, the friendliest you would ever meet, either buying or selling their hand-me-downs, jewelry, or other crafted items.

The phenomenon of Quartzite took days to experience entirely. It was not just a shopping extravaganza, but also a social event. Folks met with the friends they'd made from last year. Every night the cold desert was lit up by hundreds of campfires, as everyone gathered around, telling stories, catching up on news, and promising to make the crusade again next year to this strange and colorful Mecca.

There were over twenty campgrounds in Quartzite, empty all year but filled and overflowing in January. I pulled into one where I had not previously stayed. Although the RV park was stark with gravel landscape and rocks outlining the spaces, I was surprised to see, rising up in front of every campsite, ten-feet-tall iron sculptures of either cacti or palm trees. These sculptures were designed from old rusted horseshoes welded together. Then I noticed other statues near the office. One was a ten-feet-tall cowboy, his arms made out of large rusted wrenches, his stomach a gear from some discarded machine, and his hat an old fruit can. A twenty-foot whale of welded horseshoes at the entrance to the park made its home in a pond, with its spout acting as the fountain. Many more art figures decorated the clubhouse area: a roadrunner, an Indian poised with bow and arrow, a dog baring rusted teeth made from a gear chain. I imagined the artist creating these amazing images in his mind. I could see him gathering the old rusty tools and iron skeletons of machines long dead in order to design these magnificent forms in the middle of this hot, dry, nowhere place. His love showed strongly in these figures that took hours of sweat and pounds of weld to create. My first night on the road, and I was surrounded and warmed by the artist's inspiration. I would always remember this oasis that soothed and nourished my lonely soul.

I backed The Wizard into my assigned spot easily and then performed my RV duties of plugging in the electrical cord, hooking up the water and sewer hoses, and positioning the satellite dish. All my practice at those nearby campsites, before my attempting this ultimate trip, had paid off. Jack Incarnate just stared into space, enraptured by the cactus sculpture in front of him. Sportster had decided the place needed his inspection and sat patiently by the screen door, waiting for what would become an evening ritual: a walk, a cat walk. I fastened his Harley leash to his jeweled harness, carried him outside, and set him down on the patio, snapping his leash to a twelve-pound boat anchor that served as a tie-down. Sportster spent the first five minutes rolling and twisting on the rough concrete. He then used the next thirty minutes taking his "walk," which involved methodically sniffing every inch of the campsite within the radius of his taut leash.

Meanwhile I relaxed on my recliner lawn chair and unwound with a cup of coffee while I watched the desert sunset. At peace, I mentally took inventory of my day. I was safe and sound while my hurting heart whimpered with some satisfaction at the day's accomplishment, too afraid yet to be fully happy. Darkness settled in and Sportster and Iwent inside to prepare for bed. A hot shower was a must for a good night's sleep. While waiting for the water heater to finish warming, I turned down the bed. Sportster took his guard position on the dash, his cat-eyes studying creatures and bugs passing in the darkness outside.On TV, I caught the L.A. news and weather that would soon become unimportant, information that would soon become unimportant, as the days and miles from home increased.

I had promised updates of my trip to my sister Sandy, Helen, my manager, and my friend and former employee Vickie every night. (My final destination was Vickie's home in Florida.) First call was to Helen, who reported the day's business and assured me that everything was running smoothly on my first day away. Sandy, was my next call, and with pride I announced that I had traveled two hundred and fifty miles with no incidents.

I was tired but victorious. It was decided that each day, I would give her the campground's name, city, and state, in the event that I was never seen again, so she would know where to start her search. She and Vickie were the worriers in my life now that Jack was gone—it took two worriers to replace him, since he had been such an intense one. After placing my last call to Vickie, my fretful team was reassured for the night with information of my route and destination for tomorrow. Suddenly I felt like I might as well be a million miles from home because I was now officially on my own.

My first night on the road. I could feel the aloneness on my skin, my skin that will never feel Jack's touch again, or, I was sure, anyone else's. I shivered as I imagined a stranger's touch, because I couldn't imagine anyone who would not be a stranger to me. So I was alone as I peered out into the darkness of the campground and noted the warm light of togetherness glowing behind the shades of every RV. Flickers of TV light bounced inside the cozy interiors. End-of-the-day conversations mixed with plans of Thanksgiving floated in the air, while the aromas of everyday dinners cooked with love delighted the senses. By ten o'clock a hush came over the campground. The quiet was soothing, even in my aloneness. I felt at peace knowing and remembering that I'd had my experience and enjoyed my time. The couples here were now having theirs. There was a time and a season for everything.

In bed now with the darkness, as I gazed at the stars in the clear night sky, I felt Sportster jump up to join me. He padded across the covers, sat attentively near my head, and gently reached his paw out to touch my face. His tenderness made me want to believe that he had read my read my lonely thoughts and offered comfort: *I'm here for you, Mom.* I massaged his neck, burying my fingers into his soft fur and listening to his purring sound of contentment. How could I feel down, with this little guy showing me the only kind of love I could handle right now, cat love? Although cat love is not without conditions such as food, water, and pats and scratches, these conditions I could meet. I pulled his whiskered face to mine and inhaled his scent as I gave him a big kiss that he stiffly tried to slough off. He then crawled under the bedsheets and curled into a warm, vibrating ball next to my skin. Road dust washed away, my tummy filled, and lights out; my first day on the road was now completed successfully. With one stitch of confidence and courage sewn into my bleeding heart, I drifted off, the sound of the interstate in the distance lulling me to sleep.

I dreamt of childhood family road trips, when we'd head southwest from my home state of Illinois. Route 66 was the mother road at that time, carrying the traveler through hundreds of miles of pristine mountain, desert, and small-town landscape. Quite often the small towns were the only civilization for hundreds of miles and endless hours, until we reached the next small town. Those long miles and hours between towns were very trying for two pre-teen girls full of energy, whose parents tried to keep childish arguments from escalating. When everyone needed a break, Dad would steer our Willy's Jeep and attached travel trailer under a big shade tree alongside the road. That would be our rest stop. No sooner than had the tires came off the asphalt and hit the gravel, my sister and I had the Jeep's doors open, and we would hit the ground running.

I dreamt of the lunch stops in the desert in particular. We chased lizards and horned toads, with no thoughts of rattlesnakes. I didn't even remember parental warnings about them. We were young and had no fears. Most nights were spent at these "natural" rest stops. There were no streetlights here, hundreds of miles from the nearest little town, but stars made the night sky literally glow. My sister and I would lie in our bed in the darkness, peering out at the stars, giggling and whispering far into the night. I could hear the whoosh of the occasional lone car or truck that would pass by in the darkness on the highway, its headlights momentarily shining in our window and casting eerie moving shadows across the warm maple wood of the travel trailer's interior and then, just as quickly, fading away into darkness. I was sure that somewhere on one of these family trips I had developed my wanderlust, not just for any form of travel, but for road trips in particular. I knew all that was important to me in my short twelve years of life existed, safe and secure, warm and snug, in that little cocoon of a trailer, and it was the best feeling in the world.

I awakened to the new day with coffee brewing inside and Sportster browsing outside. It was a traveling day, so the RV chores included stashing and storing. And dumping, the downside of RV'ing. I donned fashionable rubber gloves, and, before I pulled the lever to release all the unpleasantness, I checked the hoses to ensure that they were secure both at the motor home tank and where the hose connected to the ground sewer. Any malfunction could cause a disastrous flood that would ruin not only my day but my neighbor's as well, making me a disgrace to the RV community. All went well as I unhooked the hoses and unplugged the electrical cord. In a final walk around my rig, I checked that the storage compartments were secure, the steps were raised, the antenna was down, and the tires inflated. Ready to roll. Sportster, sensing a new day of adventure, took his co-navigator's position on the dash. Jack Incarnate said he'd had enough of this place and was ready to move on. The Wizard roared into action eager to move on and then settled into its familiar all's-well purr. After checking the mirrors, I eased out of the site, past the rusty figures whose spirits waved me on, bidding me safe traveling.

On the road again, saying good-bye to comfortable surroundings, I set my sights for Tombstone, Arizona. The hours droned on, mixed with the sounds of travel. The traffic's rhythm rolled smoothly as colorful travel bugs in the forms of Hondas, Fords, and Hummers crept in and out of lanes, passing me and the big rigs as they scurried to their destinations. Eventually we all met up at the next rest stop and I, being the lone solo traveler, got the head start back onto the freeway. After a short time, the colorful travel bugs crept up again, scurried past, and shrank into the distance.

The traffic thickened as Phoenix neared. My grip on the wheel tightened, and I reeled my mind back from its meanderings to tend to the traffic ahead. I thought I heard Jack Incarnate grumble. I glanced over at him. Maybe not. I turned my attention back to the road, and the sight of a low-flying jetliner filled my windshield. Was it coming in for a landing or was it in trouble? It was so close, I was afraid for having such a high-profile vehicle. The traffic ahead moved at a normal pace, so I assumed that the jet was landing on a runway parallel to the interstate. My panic passed, and I moved on through the city limits, reading the billboards like pages of a tour book: one promised casinos with loose slots and fast wins, another guaranteed the Best Night of Rest for Less. Of course there were the reminders(Macdonald's, Next Exit), the campgrounds that bragged of resort lifestyles, and the five-star restaurants that stirred my appetite. By the time I had reached the city's limit, I was feeling deprived that I was not indulging in everything Phoenix had to offer.

Next stop, Tombstone, Arizona, the town "too tough to die," home of Wyatt Earp, the OK Corral, and Boot Hill. History hung around this town and leaned its stories up against every gas lamppost like a cowboy, kicked back, hat tilted, rolling a cigarette. Millions of tourists came from around the world to experience the history that was reenacted every hour at the OK Corral.

The town got its name from a soldier named Sheffield, who was stationed at Camp Huachuca (now Fort Huachuca) in 1877. He had left the camp to prospect for gold and silver. His fellow soldiers laughed and told him the only thing he would find was his tombstone. When he made his silver discovery, he named his claim "Tombstone," in remembrance of their taunts. His discovery began a rush of silver mines, and the town of Tombstone flourished in lawlessness until 1881, when Wyatt Earp and Doc Holliday brought back civilization with the famous shoot-out at the OK Corral.

I discovered a small campground on Allen Street, which is the main street of Tombstone and two blocks from the OK Corral. I backed in, plugged in, and hooked up. It was late afternoon as I settled into my recliner to watch Sportster sniffing the scents of his pioneer ancestors. Hearing *clip, clop, clip, clop* sounds growing near, I watched as a team of horses pulling a stagecoach came into view. Sportster, too, saw these dinosaur-sized creatures and made a frightened dash for the safety of the motor home's interior. I jumped up quickly and opened the door as he scrambled to some hidey-hole inside. I waved to the tourists inside the stagecoach as the horses made a U-turn, heading back to town. Stillness settled in again, and

Sportster reappeared from his hiding spot. Every hour, this amusing scene repeated itself: the clip clopping, Sportster's mad dash for safety, my wave, the U-turn, and then quiet again.

A middle aged couple stepped out of the Cruise America motorhome that was parked next to me. Following behind them was their son who was probably abought eight years old. As they passed by the Wizard I noticed the boy poke his dad motioning to my motorhome's interior. The parents stopped and glanced up and they all laughed. I rose from my chair and stepped closer.

"Hi there! My guy never has much to say but he is great travel partner. He never complains and he doesn't eat much." They all chuckled and I noticed the boy still staring closely. I don't know if he was fully convinced that Jack Incarnate was only a doll. "Would you like to meet him?" The boy's eyes got big and a hesitant smile crossed his face as he looked up to his folks questioningly.

His dad chuckled, "Sure go ahead."

I unlocked the door and lifted Jack Incarnate out of the passenger seat, sitting him in the lounge chair so the boy could examine him better although his parents were just as eager to meet him.

"He's a Harley man but he left his bike at home. And he wears the Harley hat to hide his bald head. See?" I lifted the cap to expose his bald head and pony tail. Everyone laughed in unison. "And he's got a lot of money too. Look at his watch and ring." I lifted up his fabric arm so they could better observe his jewelry.

"Wow. He is really something! We thought he was real at first." The mom had an accent, German maybe. "That is good because you are alone, right? So people think you have a partner, huh?"

"Yes but he is more entertaining than anything. I sure meet a lot of people because of him. Where are you folks from?"

"We are from Frankfurt, Germany and are on a holiday. We have heard do much about your Hollywood and Western movies that we had to see for ourselves.We have heard about, how do you say, ' the shootout at the OK Corral?"

Now it was my turn to laugh. "Well you are in the right place."

"This is my wife Helga and my boy, Erich. My name is Herm." He reached out and I shook his hand.We visited a little more and they invited me to accompany them on the two block walk into town.

"Sure let me just get Jack Incarnated tucked back inside and lock up. I have a cat too. Oh there he is on the dash. See him?" the boy pulled his attention away from Jack Incarnate as I was stuffing him back into the passenger seat. The lad's face lit up when he saw Sportster. "When you get back tonight you can meet Sportster," I promised.

It wasfew hours before sundown, when the town would roll up its streets, so I did a little shopping and experienced the reenactment of the shoot-out. . I bought a poster of Wyatt, Doc, and their gang with the famous quote from the movie, *Tombstone*, "I'm comin' and Hell's comin' with me." Wow! Those were the days when things got done. I picked up brochures in town, discovering that this area was definitely a place to spend some time. The points of interest were many: the Fort Huahuca, the mining town of Bisbee (including a tour of its nearby copper mine, the Kartcher Caverns), and Cochise's Stronghold, to name just a few.

When I returned from my shopping, I again made my phone calls. Only two calls tonight to Sis and Vickie, because it was Sunday and the shop was closed. Sandy was relieved to hear from me as I reported the little incidents of the day and my shopping finds in Tombstone. Exchanging "I love yous," we said good night. Vickie too had relief in her voice as I reported that I was now five hundred miles closer to her. I reassured her all was going well and I was having the time of my life. After saying good-bye, I hesitantly admitted to myself that, yes, I really was having the time of my life. How many people would like to be doing what I was but were unable, either because of finances or physical disabilities? I felt so blessed, but still my heart continued to remind me with each beat that it was unhappy on this venture because it had to survive alone, unaccompanied by its long-time partner.

It was early morning daylight as I left Tombstone. In the dawn's light a doe sprang across the narrow road and disappeared into the brush. I passed Boot Hill and silently thanked the souls who unknowingly shared their lives with me. The ghosts of Wyatt and Doc waved me on, and I was sure that I saw Jack Incarnate nod in response as we passed Boot Hill. Didn't his cloth hand touch his hat in salute? Maybe not.

Chapter Three

As Tombstone's souls vanished into the fog on my rearview mirror, my thoughts flashed back to the first time I'd met Jack. He would play country singer Don Williams's song, "I Believe in You" on the jukebox, over and over, to get my attention when he was trying to win my heart at an AA club where we both attended meetings. The club had a bar atmosphere, but there was no alcohol, and only coffee was served at the "coffee "bar." Al-Anon and AA meetings were conducted throughout the day and evenings. Dances and potlucks were organized on holidays, giving the recovering alcoholic and the family a place to socialize without the temptation of alcohol. I attended Al-Anon meetings, and occasionally AA meetings, to help me deal with the alcoholics in my life. Jack had been sent to the club by the court system after he had been arrested on his second drunk-driving offense. The judge in Jack's case had discovered that AA meetings were quite effective, and had sentenced many second-time offenders to AA meetings instead of jail time.

Jack showed up at the AA club on a day when I had just been hanging out, having a cup of coffee. He had his card from the court in hand, which he would get signed as proof that he had attended a meeting. Usually the courts required ten or more meetings. I could see he was nervous, as were most newcomers, so I offered to go with him to the meeting. We sat through that meeting together, and, little did I know, that was the beginning of the day I lost my heart.

Jack told me months later that the day he had seen me at the coffee bar was the day he fell in love with me. He told me he took one look at me and said, "These meetings are not going to be so bad." He'd asked the other guys around the coffee bar who I was. They told him, "Oh that's Judy. You don't want to mess with her. She's one of them." many of the male alcoholics at the club said that because they considered me "an Al-Anon," not an alcoholic. There was a continuing underlying dissension, and a lot of joking and teasing, between these two factions. The Al-Anon member was usually the wife of the alcoholic, and, by the time these people got to the doors of the AA club and the meetings to deal with their addictions, there were often serious problems in the marriages or relationships. So the Al-Anon member was jokingly referred to as "the enemy," since the Alcoholicswere most likely forced to go to meetings to avoid divorce or separation. But of course Jack was not aware of all these nuances, so when they informed him that I was "one of them," he thought they meant that I was gay, and he said to himself, "I can fix that!" I have always admired that he was not a quitter. When he wanted something, he latched on like a pit bull and would not let go. Thank goodness. I was not that easy to win over.

Jack was an urban cowboy but I could never get him to wear the hat. He had never seen the back of a horse but had paraded the streets of L.A. in every style of muscle car, and laid rubber with every Triumph and Harley he owned. His baby face complemented small baby-blue eyes and narrow lips, with skin as soft and smooth as a baby's. He wore a fifties ducktail, and tight, hot-looking jeans hung from his slim hips. The tattoos from his arms to his smooth Cherokee chest were like petroglyphs speaking of past women's names and other life events that only he could interpret.

He was tough, oh so tough, taught at an early age not to expose his soft puppiness. That secret softness is what I loved about him, a hidden aspect that no one else knew about him. In private he could cry when he was touched by tenderness. And he knew right from wrong. If you were wrong, you were dead wrong. You treat your mother with respect even if she didn't always do right by you. Children had their own very special place in the universe, never to be disillusioned or abused, always to be cherished and honored. I wondered how often he'd brought his own personal justice to the misguided souls in jail who had failed to meet his personal code of honor code. He had done numerous stretches of time for drinking, fighting, and for being too tough as he aspired to his drunken father's image of what a man should be.

Jack became a man at seven years old when one day he'd come home from school crying, not because he had been beaten up in a fight, but because during that fight they had torn his shirt that his mother had made. His father, always in a state of drunkenness, became enraged by his crying and was not going to have a weakling for a son. "I am going to teach this boy a lesson," he told Jack's terrified mother, who begged, "Please, leave him alone." The small boy, still sniveling, further angered his father, who dragged Jack to the garage and taught him a lesson he would never forgot. Jack grew up that day, bit by painful bit, each time his father flung him up against the garage walls, every time his father beat him with angry, drunken fists, over and over. He decided that day he would rather take beatings from the kids at school. He could survive those, but never again would he show weakness to his father or anyone else, because he just might not live through another beating like the one he received that day. No one ever saw him cry again.. The alcohol that his father allowed him, even at that young age, soothed his loneliness.

So that was my cowboy, who had set his sights on me that day. Tougher than anyone I ever knew. Even then I unconsciously knew I would be safe and he would always have my back, that he would love me and only me. That day, the draw had been made. I would eventually surrender to his earth-quaking charm as it crumbled the wall around my own heart. That day my broncobuster had already mounted up and cast his lariat, before I even knew I had been lassoed. It was going to be a wild adventurous ride, with jerking twists and jarring turns.

Jack, who cared passionately about life but had tried to smother his feelings with alcohol, decided to end his alcoholic road trip. My own lonely road, which allowed me to escape from caring by never getting close to any one, came to a screeching halt as well. And there we were, making eyes at one another at the AA club's coffee bar. I had often wondered how, in God's infinite wisdom, He had orchestrated these events to occur in such perfect sequence as to form a defining moment. But He did that day. Jack and I locked eyes and the heavens swirled above our heads, sprinkling fairy dust onto our hearts. Jack felt the potency of the magical dust far more than I did, so the age-old courting dance began.

At the moment these recollections were fading in my rearview mirror as I cruised east on I-10. They would spring on me again around the next curve, like the wind gusting into an open window. Some gusts of memories could be bitingly cold, and others scorched my emotions, but they all would transport me to places I thought had vanished into eternity. Other pleasant thoughts would drift in like a balmy breeze, their visits delighting me.

Leaving Tombstone and entering the interstate, I settled into the tedium of travel just as it began to rain. The drops pattered my windshield and produced a shower sound on the roof. The fresh smell of wet asphalt soaked the air and the whooshing of the wipers kept rhythm with the song of the tires in the rain. The storm became heavy at times, causing the semi in front of me to morph into a cloud of moisture. My mood became dreary and gray as the skies dampened my spirits.

Once again my thoughts cascaded down a rapid river of memories. My life with Jack was like a rafting trip, with terrifying white water I thought I would never live through, and then, just around the bend, serene smooth-as-glass water that lulled and restored my soul.

I sank into those baby-blue eyes. They were small pools, summer ponds reflecting the color of the sky. I would live there forever in those eyes that touched me somewhere deep. Jack's face was soft, his lips warm, and the air I breathed was full of him, filling my lungs with a yielding weakness. My heart ached with submission. It would stop beating for this man if he asked. I could not move as his lips softly brushed mine. The touch sent searing hot jolts ripping through me, and I plummeted into surrender.

With that one kiss, the playful, carefree courtship was over. He asked gently, "Are you sure?" I had no choice; I was a puddle of desire. I didn't,

I couldn't think. I nodded. Our souls, molten with lust, entwined and solidified: we were one. The blissful night sang us to sleep and, at morning's light, I knew he would be there forever.

At dawn we headed for Las Vegas with our hopes and dreams packed in our overnight bags. Jack's truck had a cab-over-camper with a bed, sink, and a two-burner stove, but no bathroom. The road to Vegas was long with few distractions. Our wedding trip offered us plenty of time to think and dream, but never a moment to consider the reality of it all.

We stopped at a country-style diner, atop Cajon Pass, that was a favorite of big rigs. Breakfast was friendly waitresses, smiling young couples, and loud-talking family groups, all mixed in with unshaven truckers in cowboy boots. Everyone was traveling their separate journeys, unconscious of their unity in this one moment in time. With full tummies we climbed back into the truck, and I slid across the bench seat to snuggle with this man with whom I would share the next twenty-five years, in sickness and health, for richer or poorer, 'til death did us part.

It was my first time in Las Vegas, and the neon lights flashed to the rhythm of my excited heartbeat. Only in Vegas did the fever of the desert flare into a frenzy and hurl its visitors into the illusion of a magical land of enchantment. Nothing seemed real. Neon colors painted the night with garish colors. The cool night air disguised the punishing heat of yesterday and tomorrow. Women walking the street enticed men with a promise of love, but delivered, for a week's pay, only a memorable hour.

Then there were the sounds of Vegas. Bells ringing atop slot machines, announcing winners as beacons flashed. Screams of delight couldn't muffle the sound of coins clinking into metal trays. Loud commands to the dice could be heard at crap tables over the delicate plinking of the little white ball as it danced on the roulette wheel. Eyes became frozen stares as the tiny sphere made its whimsical, be-bopping journey around and around, finally coming to rest.

This was Vegas. The hoochie coochie long legged show girls in feathers and furs and glitter and glitz. The Rat Pack and Wayne Newton. And the high-stakes poker players, whose antes were a fortune for the average Joe, in the tense quiet corners. Las Vegas was a buffet, a steak or breakfast for $1.99. And finally, Vegas was the wedding capital of the world. Every five hundred feet was a wedding chapel. We chose *The Hitching Post Wedding Chapel*. Within minutes we were united in matrimony and sent off with coupons for free drinks and a photo at the Lucky Lady Casino. What a deal! After our drinks, and with our photo clutched to my breast, we headed back to the truck, ready to face reality as Mr. And Mrs. Jack Howard.

Now life was full of love and hope. No more lonely days, no more heart-empty nights. We went on long walks and laughed into the night. Love flowed, sparked, flourished, and spread, until its heat was everywhere.

But slowly the togetherness began to close in. We ate together, shopped together, worked together, and played together. There was no room anymore. The spaces got smaller and the air we breathed got tighter. Tenseness and dissatisfaction pushed into the crowded space and began to feed anger and jealousy. There was trouble in paradise.

There was no turning back now. He had known from the beginning, the defining moment of that first kiss, but I was afraid too late. I told him now that maybe I wasn't sure, maybe this was not for me. He left, I begged him back. I ran, but I couldn't go far. I was filled with overwhelming feelings swirling in my head and I could not let him go. The ups and downs of my roller-coaster emotions fueled him with resentment and fear. If I was too long returning from an errand, he became distraught. I wanted to visit girlfriends, but he couldn't stand my absence. I was angry but raised to stuff it. Jack voiced his anger and I perceived him out of control. Our differences magnified with his fear of not knowing how I felt and, my fear of knowing how he felt. I felt cornered and frightened and wanted to leave. He felt angry and frightened that I would indeed leave.

The day came when I could stuff no more into my bag of unexpressed emotions. I grabbed my car keys and purse, and, just as quickly, Jack ripped them from my grasp and threw me to the floor. "You are not going anywhere." Stark terror seized me as I tried to understand the situation. Slowly, while he was already apologizing for his violent attempt to control me, I pulled myself up from the floor. I knew the apology did not grant my escape, but I allowed him to comfort me. All he wanted was for me to stay, but now he had made it worse. Now, he too was terrified because he knew he had frightened me. He threatened me. "You'd better not call the cops." We were both terrified, with no way out.

He struggled to make it better. Talking softly, touching gently, he tried to take me to a better place, when our love was untainted. I closed my eyes and thought of a safer place. The night that never ended became daylight. Calmer now, Jack allowed me to leave. I went directly to my neighbor's and called the police. When the officers arrived, they did not arrest Jack but convinced him to leave, and I returned to the house.

My mind was now racing between rage and fear. Jack's ominous threat now haunted me. I had called the police but they did nothing. I marched down to the station and spoke to the officers' superior, I convincing him that a crime had been committed. He wrote a report and issued an arrest warrant, but Jack had disappeared with his bags of loss and betrayal.

I hid in the darkened room, the phone to my ear. My entire body shook uncontrollably as sweat leaked down my temple. The officer at the other end must have heard my voice trembling. I felt like a dried leaf clinging to a branch, hoping to hang on as the cold harsh wind blew cruelly against my brittle spine. The voice at the other end tried to calm me: "We are on the way. Our ETA is five minutes, four minutes...." There was every reason to stay calm, to trust. But trust, from so long ago, lured me into this darkened room with the shades drawn and the sunlight peeking through the edges. Trust had made me blind to common sense. Blind to what had erupted in this room, destroying everything. I prayed they got there in time. It didn't really matter when they arrived because everything was gone. The trust was gone. It was already over. It was too late.

Jack's instincts from years of dealing with angry women screamed that it was a trap. But his heart wanted to see me. Hope pulled him in to patch things up. "I'm on my way." The sinking feeling must have permeated the truck's cab as he turned the corner. It was too late. Police surrounded him. He had sensed the ambush, but he loved me and couldn't say no to my deceitful plea. He climbed down from the cab with his hands on his head and dropped to his knees. A violent shove from behind forced his body to the ground. His face felt the heat of the asphalt at the same time the cold muzzle of the shotgun pushed against the back of his damp neck. After a search of his truck and the reading of his rights, it was over quickly. The corner by my house was empty and quiet.

The voice on the other end of the line said, "We have him. He is in custody." I collapsed to my knees in desperate relief and, just as the last ounce of terror left me, I sprang up like a see-saw as a new fear gripped me: What if he made bail?

The arraignment was closed to the public because of the sensitivity of the charges: imprisonment, spousal abuse, and rape. If he were charged, he would be facing twenty-five years to life. He listened to the prosecutor's questions and my answers. I felt small and frightened in the massive mahogany witness box.

"When he threw you to the floor and ordered you to stay, were you angry?"

"No, I was frightened."

"The next morning when he let you leave and you pressed charges against Mr. Howard, did you want to punish him?"

"No, I just wanted him to know what he had done to me. He needed to know what he did."

The questioning dragged on for over an hour as the defense attorney tried to prove I was just an angry wife trying to retaliate.

"So, you were not angry?"

"No, I was hurt and humiliated. I felt degraded."

Finally the prosecution rested and the judge's voice boomed in the closed courtroom.

"I find there is sufficient evidence to charge the defendant with all three counts, imprisonment, spousal abuse, and rape."

I watched as Jack, in heavy chains and the bright orange of prison garb, was escorted back to his cell. I had seen him listen to the pounding interrogation of his defense attorney and flinch at each of my trembling answers. Before he turned the corner, I could feel his heart was heavy with regret and fear For the first time in his miserable life he was sober, but in jail and facing twenty-five years to life. He was scared. What happened? He loved that woman. How could he have done what he did? Now he had lost everything. Before her, he had nothing, but she was everything, a promise of life and love that he had searched for his entire life. Now it was all gone. It was over.

Alone in the filth and stench of his cell, this tough, tattooed Harley man fell down to his knees and prayed to a God not of his own understanding.

"*If there is a way to mend this*.... *Please... because I am powerless.*"

He paid no heed to the other prisoners who, sensing his vulnerability, were ready to attack like a pack of wolves. That day, he gave up. The fight left him and he accepted God's will, not knowing what that might be.

It was early morning when the phone rang. He had waited two hours to get his allotted five minutes of time on the jail phone.

"Hello?"

"Judy,it's me."

"What do you want?"

"I just want you to know that I am not going to fight the charges against me. I don't want to put you through any more. I love you and I am sorry for everything. I will plead guilty."

The surrender and sorrow in his voice echoed sadly through the phone line. This was the voice of a different man. He was calm and grounded.

How could he be, in his situation? But he was. His voice was strong as he laid his heart on the line one last time.

"I am so sorry. If only I could make it up to you, I would. I am nothing without you. I will always love you, Judy. Even now."

His words touched me somewhere deep, and I knew everything was going to be okay. I don't believe I really had a choice, anyway. There was a power greater than myself now in control. Others say it was just my foolish heart, yearning for a better day and full of hope. But I heard this man make a pledge to surrender his life rather than hurt me anymore.

I called the district attorney and, like so many abused wives after hearing a little sweet talk, begged the D.A. to drop the charges. He explained tiredly, as he had probably done so many times before to similarly abused women, that the only way to stop the proceedings at this point was to talk to the judge.—and getting time with the judge before sentencing was rare. Now I was afraid that Jack would not ever get out of jail. I wanted him home and was full of faith that we could work it out.

I dressed carefully, nervous of the unknown outcome on the day of the sentencing hearing. My friend had advised me the night before that that the judge was not in charge; neither was I, nor was Jack. "Only God is in charge," she reminded me, and I clung desperately to that thought like a raft on the rapids. I arrived at the courthouse early enough to locate the courtroom before the proceedings began. I approached the bailiff with Jack's case number and asked if I could possibly to speak to the judge about dropping the charges. He explained that it was never done, but he would try to get a word with the judge. I said a silent prayer, "*Your will, not mine, God.*"

Jack shuffled into the courtroom in chains that linked him to ten other cellmates. The orange-clad group, led by the guard, moved unevenly to their seats. The bailiff approached the guard, speaking low and pointing to Jack. The guard nodded as he pulled a large batch of keys from his belt of guard gear, which included a billy club, tazer, and a large black revolver. Walking over to Jack, the guard unlocked the chains that bound him to the others.

I could see Jack's face as his mind began racing. He had been in and out of jails all his life. He knew the routine of the proceedings and that this was never done. The prisoners were never separated. He didn't know whether to be fearful or hopeful. What was happening? The bailiff led him to the judge's chamber door and knocked softly. The door opened and Jack disappeared inside. The bailiff turned and now approached me, sitting in the galley.

"Would you come with me?"

"Yes, sir."

Again the chamber door opened and I entered. There was Jack, sitting across from the judge himself.

"Please sit down," the judge ordered.

"Yes, sir." The judge's eyes bore into me.

"I don't now why I am doing this, because I have gone over Mr. Howard's case and reviewed his file. If you could see his file, you would know that it is six inches thick. I don't understand why you are requesting this, but I will take your request under consideration."

I knew why he was doing this: there was a higher power in charge! I felt a calmness overcome me. I wanted to remember this moment forever.

"Thank you, Your Honor." I rose, sneaking a quick glance into Jack's stunned face, and returned to my seat while Jack was shuffled back to his chain of prisoners. The judge came out and took his seat on the bench.

"All rise!"

"Hear ye! Hear ye! This court will come to order!" Jack's case was called.

"How do you plead?"

"Guilty, Your Honor." Jack was now at the mercy of the judge. The sentencing could go however the judge deemed.

"You will be released on one year probation with a suspended sentence and mandatory marriage counseling. If you break the terms of this probation you will serve twenty-five years." The judge then looked at me. "Make note, Mrs. Howard, that your husband has asked for the suspended sentence so you would feel safe that he would not break his probation." So Jack knew that if he slipped up in any way, he would do twenty-five years, with no trial and no second chance.

I nodded grimly. I said a silent prayer for courage. He was coming home.

Chapter Four

Suddenly I maneuvered a sharp turn, which jarred my mind back to the present. The momentum sent my memories scurrying onto the roadside, where they vanished into a whirlwind of colorful fall leaves. He was not coming home this time. He had already gone home. The distance from Tombstone increased while the rain pelted the roof and the tires parted groove-sized paths on the watery pavement. ...." I was approaching the city limits of the west Texas town of El Pasoand Marty Robbins was falling in love with a Mexican girl on the radio. El Paso wasthe sixth-largest city in Texas and the twenty-second-largest in the nation, with its skyscrapers in the foreground. The Marty Robbins song on the radio described a long-ago scene as the modern skyline loomed, the New Mexico badlands becoming its backdrop. I wondered if there is a tourist attraction called "Rosa's Cantina" somewhere on the outskirts of this metropolis. In the pounding rain, I picked my way through commuter traffic without incident and reached the city's eastern edge as the Texas sun set in the western horizon. Wanting to sigh with relief from that driving challenge and find a campground for the night, I slowed down as I approached looming orange warning lights, flashing in the growing darkness of dusk. All eastbound lanes were closed due to flooding. The tightness in my neck gripped even harder as I maneuvered the detour and returned back to a Flying J truck stop I had noticed a half-mile back.

Weary travelers were all slowly wading through the detour that herded them onto the westbound lane back to El Paso. We were all pulling into the Flying J truck stop, its parking lot filled with cars of frustrated families headed home for the holidays. There were utility trucks and big rigs fully loaded with Christmas wares that would soon stock store shelves. I found a parking space just as Jack Incarnate began to bitch. "*I told you we never should have taken this trip. What were you thinking Judy? And....*" I climbed out of the cab into a light mist of rain and heard murmurings of other travelers mulling around. I noticed a young couple in a heated conversation on the other side of the parking lot as they vented their frustration at each other about the detour. I was grateful Jack Incarnate chose to wait in the motor home. I approached an older couple standing next to their RV and asked if they had heard how long the road would be closed.

"Ther' all hopin' it will be fixed by mornin'. It looks like we all'll be spendin' the night here."

The man's southern drawl warmed the chill evening air. He reminded me of a southern gentleman with a short neatly trimmed beard and goatee. His jeans had a crisp crease down the leg front and he wore a western shirt I am sure his wife had ironed that morning. She too had white hair, short but long enough to brush her neck in a soft curl. She wore a matching blue fleece sweat suit that made her seem cuddly as she smiled brightly and suggested,

"Y'all are welcome to park next to us. You might feel safer." She nodded to where I was parked. The dust-colored van next to me seemed to be traveling its last miles on its worn rubber tires, and the four people standing alongside it had not traveled far from the drugged days of the sixties era, themselves. Welcoming the kind woman's invitation, I went back to my rig, climbed in, and prodded the the Wizardback to life It groaned with reluctance as it Pulled up next to the old couple's rig. I informed Jack Incarnate and he was not too happy about the situation. *"What if the road's not open by morning? This trip was your idea, Judy. I told you it is too far to go. What if...?"* I shut off the motor that hadn't drowned the sound of his worrisome mutterings, and stepped back outside. I decided to bypass my own cooking and and eat some "real home cookin'" while I people-watched. *"I'm not going to waste money on food when we have plenty right here in the fridge."*

"God, why doesn't he shut up?" I could still hear him through the closed door. Locking up, I left. Again I surveyed the parking lot. Glancing

around, I realized that most of these travelers would be sleeping in their cars, and I was suddenly very grateful for my home on wheels with a bathroom, a cuddly bedroom, food in the refrigerator, and, of course, Sportster. He was now engrossed in water droplets on the windshield that were lit up by the parking-lot lights, becoming laser beams as they squiggled down the glass then magically disappeared.

Inside the restaurant, seated at a large table, was a family of five, conversing among themselves as the baby steadily banged her spoon on the table. Two grungy truckers, who ate while they scratched entries in their travel logs, occupied another table. In the corner, two young lovers, their hands linked across the table, were probably journeying to celebrate their first family Thanksgiving together. After a dinner of country-fried steak, mashed potatoes, and homemade dinner rolls, I headed back to my motor home and visited with the old couple who were standing outside their rig.

"I'm Bob and this here is my wife, Janet. We are headed to Mississippi to spend Thanksgiving with our daughter and her family. We are from Bend Oregon"

After a little more small talk and joking about Jack Incarnate when I explained he was not happy about the delay, I wished them a good night, thanked them again for watching out for me, and called it a night. Thank goodness that Jack Incarnate had already fallen asleep. Sportster curled up at the foot of the bed as I, feeling safe and warm, snuggled under the covers.

Morning came with a mass exodus from the truck stop. Before I even opened my eyes, I knew that the road was open from the din of the diesels coming alive as truckers fired up their engines and rolled out to the interstate. I peeked past the bedroom shade. The weather was clear and the parking lot dry. My Mississippi neighbors were just easing past my window, heading out. I quickly dressed, cranked up the generator, and made a cup of instant coffee in the microwave. I wasn't far behind the Mississippi motor home when I hit the interstate.

Somewhere between Tombstone and El Paso I had been enticed by a billboard's advertising that a side trip to the Carlsbad Caverns should not be ignored.

I took the exit to Carlsbad Caverns. I was already yearning to explore Las Cruces and Santa Fe, New Mexico, but my focus for now was a tour of the caverns. The two-lane highway led me farther away from the interstate. The desolate Chihuahua Desert intimidated me as I encountered few vehicles. *"We shouldn't have strayed from the interstate. What if we get a flat? How far is it Judy? Do you know what can happen on a lonely road like this? What were you thinking?"* I tried to block out Jack Incarnate's fretful lecturing. A road sign timidly announced an approaching town: Malaga. Slowing, I saw what poverty looked like. The cars parked in front of a small market were vintage, and, across the road, a school and a small Catholic church were the only buildings that still showed life. Next to the church stood an adobe skeleton, staunchly refusing to die. Several one-room homes with once-upon-a- time, inviting front porches, now supported only a rickety sofa. Each was inhabited by a family of at least six, who likely worked in the surrounding, scrawny fields. The town was named after a variety of grapes that had been grown here in the 1890s by Swiss immigrants and Italian laborers. The vineyards were long gone, as was most of the town.

The next town, located just a few more miles down the road, was named Loving. It was much large,r with a population of 1,200, but it too had lost many of its historic buildings to disrepair. Oddly, a brand-new post office stood proudly. Once a year, on Valentines Day, people from around the world sent their Valentines here to this little town, just to be hand stamped, "Loving".

I arrived at Carlsbad Caverns' parking lot and Jack Incarnate, happy now, said he would stay with Sportster and enjoy the view of the Guadalupe Mountains. The tour of the caverns was uneventful. It seemed to me that everyone had someone with whom to share the experience, and the thought niggled at my sad heart. To whom will I say my oohs and aahs? They all meandered at their own pace as I set out on my own, following the path through the colorful crystal caves .. I captured the subterranean amazement of nature, in my memory and on film, to share later with Jack Incarnate, since he was always eager to hear of my adventures. An hour later, after watching a video and collecting brochures on hiking and camping in the area, I was back on the road.

Not far down the road another sign lured me to "Sitting Bull Falls." I took the turnoff, and one mile later the paved road turned to gravel and disappeared around a bend, hiding the distance to my destination. *"It was bad enough going down that lonely paved road! This is ridiculous Judy! What about the tires? Do you know how hard this is on the tires? Turn around!!"* I had gone far enough that I didn't want to turn back, so slowing, and muting the inaudible complaints from the passenger seat, I enjoyed the scenery, with the Guadalupe Mountains as a backdrop and, blessedly, no traffic. Finally, the parking lot for the falls came into view, and I saw it was occupied by quite a few travelers. I guessed I was not the only brave soul to venture to this place off the beaten pathe.

A well-marked, paved path led to the falls, but Jack Incarnate had admitted his legs were too weak to make that trek. With camera in hand, I set out alone on the short hike. The falls were delightful, and so out of character for this barren place in the Chihuahua Desert. Crystal-cool water sprayed an ethereal mist as it crashed the silence and pooled into a pond with rocks and green vegetation below. Our native ancestors surely would have christened this place sacred. But I was twenty-first-century white man, without a lot of time. I quickly captured the scene digitally and carried it back to civilization.

After having lunch with Jack Incarnate and Sportster and perusing my brochures of the Carlsbad Caverns, Sitting Bull Falls, and Lincoln National Park, I learned there were caves and other caverns to explore. Here were more "come-back-to places" to be added to my list. I headed out of the paved parking lot and traveled the few miles of gravel road back to the highway, and then the interstate. It was hard to keep my speed in check on the gravel road because I was anxious to cover some miles before dusk.

Once back on the interstate and headed back into Texas I was now, officially, on my fourth day of travel, with four states notched on my steering wheel: California, Arizona, New Mexico, and now, Texas. The rest of the day passed as I cruised through western Texas. Big boulders and vast vistas made up Texas. White, bright, sun-bleached boulders of all sizes and shapes gathered in groups to form blockades that jutted up and challenged the vastness. Smaller oxidized, burnished rocks were scattered like sprinkles of freckles on these washed-out barriers. A scrawny mesquite strained tenuously from a crevice, trying to grab a hold on this hard life. Yellow grasses hugged rocks that had crashed from a higher vantage onto the red clay earth below. Their brittle blades tickled the hard cold limestone with tenderness, even though they yearned for moisture in this beautiful, barren place. The yellows, whites, and reds all yelled across the emptiness, hoping to be heard over the quietness that was life in Texas and refusing to be swallowed up by the desert's silent sterility. Big boulders, vast vistas, and enormous ranch empires made up most of Texas.

Panoramic blue skies containing white puffy clouds looked down upon hundreds of Texas style ranches. The hearts of these ranch homesteads appeared as tiny clusters of miniature buildings at the end of long, winding dirt roads that were actually driveways. At the main road, intimidatingly massive gates of stone and intricate wrought iron boasted of Texan wealth and bravado while protecting the hard but lavish lifestyle of the ranchers within. Sometimes I would not see a Texan for hours. The only life forms were big rigs that roared past me, breaking the silence. And I saw cattle. Thousands of black and brown specks grazed quietly on a landscape of lonely wooden windmills and empty waiting corrals. The only colors to interest the eyes in this endless land were dirt brown, heaven blue, and cotton white.

With no rain in sight, the day evaporated into heat waves rising from the asphalt. Ready to wrap up my fourth day of travel, I pulled into a KOA campground in Fort Stockton. The woman in the office smiled brightly as I walked in.

"Hello. Can I help you?"

"Sure. I just need a spot for one night."

"I can help you with that. Where are yo headed?"

"Coca, Florida. I am from southern California so I still have a long way to go, huh?"

"Yes mam' you sure do. How many in your party?" She was peering out at my motorhome parked in front.

"Oh it's just me. That's Jack you are looking at. He won't cause any trouble." I could tell by her expression that she just realized he was not real and laughed.

"I'll bet he's a good traveling partner too." She was smiling even more brightly. "I knew a lady that traveled alone and every night she would put a large pair of men's shoes outside her rig's door so everyone would think she had a man inside."

Now it was my turn to laugh. "yes I guess that would work too."

"We have a continental breakfast here in the morning You are welcome to come. It is free. Our campground host provides the coffee and his wife bakes the best blueberry muffins. From 7 am til they're gone and they usually go fast."

I'll remember that but I may pull out as early as six. I still have a lot of miles to go."

I finished registering, thanked her for her kindness and I found my space. Backing in I shut off the engine and I could hear the Wizard exhale in exhaustion. . I hooked up, made a cup of coffee, and answered Sportster's pleas to go outside and check the surroundings. Stretching out in my chaise longue, my steaming Tombstone coffee mug on the fold-up table beside me, I settled in for some reading and looked forward to unwinding from the day's travel.

The peace of the campground was disturbed as a thirty-foot class-A motor home rumbled past my spot and came to a quiet stop in the street. From my chair I peered under the motor home to observe two legs in blue capris step down from the passenger door and onto the pavement. The blue capris moved around the front of the motor home. It was the wife, Director of Parking, who appeared. She moved up to the driver's window and proceeded to exchange words and sign language with the husband, Driver and Chief Director of Parking. She pointed here and there, and he gestured back within the interior shadows of the rig. After a few minutes of these gestures, she then walked briskly to the rear corner of their space.

The thirty-foot diesel pusher came back to life as its wheels turned sharply and slowly slipped backward into the space. As the Driver and Chief Director of Parking maneuvered into the spot, nearing its end, the Director of Parking stood so that she could be seen in the side mirror, and signaled him to continue inching backward. Finally she held up her palm, indicating for him to stop. The rig's motor shut down once more, and there was quiet again in the park.

Now the Driver and Chief Director of Parking made his appearance. He and the Director of Parking met on the passenger side of the rig, he and she pointing here and there. He walked to the rear of the motor home. She stood, waiting for him to come back to her. They met again, with more words and signing. The Chief Director of Parking walked once more back around the rig and climbed back into the driver's seat. The Director of Parking headed back to the rear corner again.

The motor home roared to life again. It began to move forward into the street. The entire scene repeated itself: the wheels turned sharply, the rig crept backward, the waving and signaling. This entire process repeated three times, and each time the signing became a little more agitated and the wife's appearance a little more taut. Finally, after his third attempt, the Chief Director seemed satisfied with the position of rig. Silence was restored as he shut down the diesel engine and it spurted out its last exhaust fume. Another traveler had brought his home to rest for a peaceful night or two.

Sportster and I returned to our musings. I studied the brochures found in the registration office and Sportster challenged Texas bugs until the evening turned to darkness and we had to retreat inside for dinner and bedtime.

The brochures, as usual, were full of information about the area. Fort Stockton really does have a fort. It was an active army post from 1867–1886. The city had directional signs posted throughout the campground, guiding tourists to the fort. The Anne Riggs Museum was located inside an old restored adobe hotel. The Grey Mule Saloon and the cemetery were other must-sees. But no signs were needed to bring attention to the region known as Big Bend. The town's spectacular landscape was the prelude to Big Bend National Park, encompassing 704,000 acres and 1,100 square miles! Big Bend National Park consisted of three areas: the Chisos Mountains, the Chihuahuan Desert, and the Rio Grande River. And if the national park was not enough to occupy the tourist, there were more interesting stops, like a little town called Lajitas. El Camino Del Rio, also called the River Road, on Highway 170, was known for its scenic route. Fort Davis and, finally, the Macdonald Observatory were just a few more stops to lure the tourists.

But I would consider all that tomorrow, when I was rested and refreshed. Now, I repeated my ritual of phone calls, reporting my position and destination for tomorrow, reassuring everyone and relating my stories of Carlsbad Caverns and Sitting Bull Falls. I then pulled the shades and thawed out some taco meat, chopped onions, tomatoes, and lettuce, and enjoyed Mexican cuisine as I caught CNN and reruns of *Seinfield*. Sportster crunched in his dish, begged for faucet water, and proceeded to curl up between my feet on the couch. If I could bottle the feeling of contentment that I got watching him sleep, I would be rich because it would be the best natural tranquilizer on the market. It was not long before my eyelids were drooping. I cleaned up my little kitchen, turned back the bed covers, and took a long hot shower. I crawled into bed as Sportster awoke from his spot on the couch. He arose, stretching into his yoga arch, then nimbly jumped off the couch to the floor, stuck it, and sailed back up onto the bed in one graceful motion.

Morning and coffee opened my eyes to the spectacular surrounding landscape of the campground, stirring a burning desire to see Big Bend National Park. Jack Incarnate cheered, "*head 'em up and roll 'em out*," after I completed packing up and stowing away, unhooking and unplugging.

The Spanish called it *Terra Desconocida*, meaning "the strange unknown land" that makes up Big Bend, where the Chihuahuan Desert met the southwest Rocky Mountains. I cruised along the long lonely road that led to the entrance of the national park, enjoying the desolateness, passing only an occasional vehicle. A road sign announced Lajitas and Terlingua Ghost Town to the right. Feeling adventurous, I made the turn, even though it was the opposite way to the park's entrance. I passed by the ghost town, because the village consisted of only a few adobe structures: La Sirena Gallery, La Posada Milagro Guesthouse for tourists staying outside the park, and an old abandoned gas station. Ten miles down the road I came upon Lajitas, population one hundred, and pulled into The Trading Post, a small market that seemed to be the heart of the town. Half a dozen vehicles lined the parking lot. As I climbed out of my rig to enter the market, I heard talking and laughter from the back of the parking lot. Curiosity lured me away from the market's front entrance, and, sauntering around the corner of the building, I approached a crowd of people gathered around a shabby enclosure of chicken wire and old wood slats that penned a black mountain goat A nicely hand-carved plaque hung on the rickety fence: "Clay Henry III". I watched in amazement as a tourist standing by the pen offered "Clay" a bottle of beer. The billy goat grabbed the bottle, his teeth gripping the glass, then rocked his head back and chugged. Emptying the suds, the goat spat the bottle aside and moved down the fence, where the next tourist fed him his next beer.

I stood to the back of the crowd and asked a young couple what was going on. They explained that the goat's name was Clay Henry Junior. His father was Clay Henry Senior, the original beer-drinking goat. Because he increased tourism in Lajitas, Clay Sr. was loved so much that in 1986 he was elected mayor. People would come for miles around, bringing a case and going toe-to-hoove drinking with him. "Posters are on sale in the Trading Post picturing Clay Senior in mid-guzzle," the old man explained.

I watched Clay Jr. chug down a few more beers and then headed into the Trading Post, where the owner held a few tourists' attention as he explained the shocking death of Clay Sr. in 1992. "Clay Senior and Clay Junior both got soused in the same pen during rutting season. Clay Junior killed his father in a drunken brawl over a female: he now drinks to forget." The owner advised tourists to see this spectacle in the morning because, "by mid-afternoon," he explained, "Clay Junior's pen is littered with empties, and he's clearly adrift in Sot's Bay. After staggering over to his salt lick, and working it furiously, he drops to all four knees while his eyes roll back in his head and he is finished." Outside I saw other goats, staggering in the parking lot after getting their fill of the Lone Star longnecks originally purchased by tourists for Clay Jr. The owner had preserved Clay Sr. by having him stuffed by a taxidermist, thenstood the old goat proudly by the register. The owner shook his head in resignation at the other goats outside. "Clay Senior used to drink as many bottles of beer as people would feed him. Clay Junior is not the goat his father was."

I bought a Coke and hung out for a while, listening to the stories about Clay Henry III, who at the time was also the mayor of Lajitas. The goat was attacked and castrated by a local in 2002, who was angry that the animal had been drinking on a Sunday, when the area's blue laws prevented the sale of alcohol. Ranchers who found the goat stitched him up. The local was charged with animal cruelty.

"The current Clay Junior now drinks thirty-five to forty beers a day," the owner continued. "He had a bit role in *The Streets of Larado* television series, and was filmed for a Sally Jesse Raphael segment in 1995. Clay Senior lived to be twenty-two, so I expect Clay Junior to be around for a while. Beer kills you, but it does it slow."

And with that I topped off my Coke and headed back to the Wizard. I relayed the stories to Jack Incarnate as we drove along, looking for a campground. He chuckled. *"I know how those goats must feel."* A little farther down the road, I found a campground and visitor center. I checked in and again gathered brochures of the area. The office clerk informed me I was the only rig in the campground besides the campground hosts, who were parked in the far corner and, she explained, were two elderly ladies. I drove to my assigned site and, after plugging into the electrical, realized I still had no electricity. I told Jack Incarnate to sit tight, and I walked back to the visitor center. The clerk told me that she would send someone to take a look at the electrical box. I had no soonergotten back to my rig than I saw two workers driving over in a golf cart. In short order the problem was resolved and all was well. But Jack Incarnate had suddenly perked up and began an ominous chant, *"I don't like that—those workersy know that we're alone. Those two little old ladies probably can't even hear. There is no one around. I don't like it, Judy, I don't like it at all."*

It was early evening and the sun was just setting on the Chisos Mountians. After setting up the satellite dish, I went outside for a quick walk with Sportster and my camera. The area was beautiful and I yearned to go for a longer walk, but dusk was turning to darkness and I could see Jack Incarnate looking around nervously. I urged Sportster back inside, locking the door behind us. This time I agreed with Jack Incarnate. We were quite isolated. When I called my sister and told her of my nervousness, she would not hang up until I retrieved my thirty-eight revolver from its hiding place and laid it within easy reach, on the counter. We both felt safer when she hung up. I then relaxed with my brochures while I feasted on chili and cornbread.

With comfort food in my tummy and Sportster crouched on the dash keeping guard, I watched the L.A. news that was of no consequence to me in Texas—but the familiarity of the places and people calmed me as I waited for the water heater to do its job. After cleaning up the kitchen and showering, I was soon tucked in bed, reading a good book. It was very quiet and very dark. Sportster had abandoned his guard post and retired to his deserved spot under the covers. The thirty-eight reassured me from its spot, within reach, on the counter. Morning came with no incident.

Some love Big Bend for its solitude, while others hate it for the same reason. I loved it. *Cole Porter whispered in my ear "Give me room, lots of room, where the west commences . . .don't fence me in.".* I had arisen early and was on the road by daybreak. As I drove through Big Bend's entrance, the sound of silence was so loud it covered the motor's hum like a soft blanket of snow. An chipmunk scurried across the road into the shade and protection of sagebrush, as his predator, a hawk, high above, floated lazily in the infinite Texas atmosphere.

An hour of stillness hovered over the road as it led through the park and into the campground. Sparse life brought small sounds of civilization as I entered. A market and registration office, a gas pump alongside, were the only amenities. A dog barking from a faraway campsite, and a nearby gas pump clicking as it fed a ranger's truck were the only soft sounds that invaded the solitude.

I checked in, registered, and, before finding my space, decided the Wizard needed nourishment and filled up with gas. The ranger at the registration office had informed me there was no cell phone reception and given me directions to a turnoff about a quarter of a mile down the road, up a hill, and on a dirt road. There I would get reception. I made a mental note but knew I would not take the Wizard down a dirt road. A couple, standing nearby, heard the ranger's explanation, walked over, and introduced themselves as Rick and Linda. "We have a Jeep and are going to that spot in the morning to make calls. You're welcome to ride along, if you'd like." Always surprised by people's kindness, I thanked them, got their space number, and made a tentative date for ten the next morning.

There were only electrical and water hookups, so I quickly set up and then proceeded to get the satellite dish out and position it. Once again, with my chair and little table unfolded and holding a cup of coffee, Sportster and I sat out watching the campgrounds activity. My neighbor's motor home towed a trailer loaded with a very small bright red car—so small, it was cute. When the couple came wandering out of their rig, I struck up the usual conversation. "Hi, where are you from?" They were from New Jersey, and of course I commented on their unusual car. The husband proudly explained it was a prototype for a new car being produced all over Europe called "The Smart Car for Two." He described all of the car's features and benefits, and I told him that I was sure it would sell just because it was so cute. I learned later I was privileged to view the first Smart Car in the States.

The couple on the other side of me was from Tennessee. They had both been laid off their jobs and were heading to family in California to start over. Sportster soaked up the usual attention from the campers as they admired a cat on a leash. He rubbed up against legs, tail straight as an arrow, and then proceeded to flop onto the ground, rolling on his back to expose his soft furry belly for rubbing. Cat people understood the antics and obliged him, while others just watched with fascination. After I felt that we both got our fill of socialization after a long day on the road, I set Sportster inside with Jack Incarnate, who, being an avid car freak, wanted to inspect the Smart Car. I felt I had been to enough car shows with Jack when he was alive; I did not need to cater to Jack Incarnate's whims. I said no. He was pouting as I left and locked the door to go exploring around the campground.

There were warnings posted around the park to keep pets leashed because of the javelinas. Javelinas belong to the pig family, are usually three to four feet in length, and can weigh up to eighty pounds. They have also been called razorback hogs and, although they mainly eat vegetation, they can be very aggressive toward humans and pets if threatened. Behind the campground I discovered a rippling creek spattered with golden leaves floating in its dark waters. The deep black water glistened with silver sparkles of filtered afternoon sunlight.

I passed many hiking trails that made me yearn for the luxury of time. I was beginning to realize on this trip that there were endless "come back to" places to visit. The brochures of this area informed the tourist of Jeep tours that would take you to waterfalls, Indian camps, abandoned mining towns, and Comanche Creek.

Finishing my stroll, I headed back to my campsite. Out of the corner of my eye, I noticed a mother javelina with four of her children marching steadfastly behind her in single file along the creek bed. They were at least fifty yards away from me, and I didn't think I was a threat. But a coyote was also following, perhaps ten feet behind the family procession. I watched with amazement for surely the coyote, the javelina's predator, was stalking the babies. The coyote and pigs all disappeared from my view, and I continued my walk. I stopped at the office and found the ranger and told him what I had witnessed. "Surely that coyote is going to kill those babies," I said, more a question than a statement.

He laughed. "Oh, don't you worry about those babies. There is nothing meaner and faster than a mother javelina protecting her young. That coyote won't have a chance if he tries to make his move."

Back at my rig and hungry, I decided that barbeque ribs, baked potato, and green beans were a must for my Texan mood. I was so grateful for all the preparation I had done for this trip as I enjoyed the barbeque aromas emanating from the microwave. I started to make my calls and then recalled the ranger's words, "no cell phone reception." I placed the phone on the charger and neatly set my little table, then perused my brochures and watched the L.A. news. My ribs and baked potato were to die for, and life was good. Jack Incarnate didn't eat a bite. He didn't realize what he was missing. Sportster took his usual evening position on the dash watching whatever only cats see with their night vision. Cleaning up my tiny kitchen, I turned down the bedcovers, which signaled Sportster to leap from his post down to the floor, stick it, and then sweep up onto the bed in his signature Olympic move. Finding his spot smack in the middle of the bed, he curled into his bedtime ball and purred into oblivion. Leaving the windows open, I pulled the shades on the darkness, shutting out Texas, the Smart Car, javelinas, and coyotes.

The night air was cold with autumn. After a steamy hot shower with the lights out, I carefully tried to climb over Sportster, but he awoke from his slumber with a disgruntled grumble. Sleeping with Sportster on a cold night was the same as having the softest, warmest electric blanket caressing me. It was like being a little girl again in pink-flowered flannel pj's and sleeping with a favorite doll. Like Sportster, the doll loved only me and understood all my little-girl dreams, as I lay alone in the dark with the black night sounds surrounding me.

Sportster's perception of his time with me was different from my view of the time I spent with him. My time with him was full of love and caring. My heart swelled with admiration at his coat's colors of whites and grays interlaced with blacks and whites. An hour could pass as I studied his calmness and gracefulness in amazement. I felt his warm, flannel-soft fur on my skin and listened to the easy humming sound of his feline motor idling until complete sleep engulfed him, carrying him into a realm free of responsibilities and obligations. Gazing at him calmed me like a scene of mirror-like water that reflected green pine-sloped mountains capped with sheets of cold snow.

Sportster's time with me was totally different. He jumped onto the bed, carefully checking every lump and wrinkle in the covers. Inspecting every inch, he searched for that perfect spot that would best suit his comfort. He then sat staring at me, his "keeper." One or two meows were enough to an adequate keeper to communicate his wants. I was trained well and lifted the covers. He remained sitting, but now began his examination under the covers as to what might be "The Spot." I patiently waited for him to mosey under and curl into a fur ball on his perfectly selected spot next to me, his prized, personal human possession. He had been born for these comforts. They were expected. Thus he purred until sleep shut down his motor and he slipped off into dreamless, well-deserved contentment.

Sometime in the very darkest of the night, I awoke. Unsure of the cause, I lay still, with my eyes still closed. And then I felt it. A featherlike touch to my face made my eyes spring wide open in alertness. For one quick heartbeat, my mind filled with fear and then just as quickly sighed with relief. There in the darkness sat Sportster, his soft fur paw retracting from my cheek as he stared intently at me. The greatest mystery with owning a cat was to interpret what it desired. A little irritated, and having no clue, I was now wide awake. This campground, like all campgrounds in the middle of the night, was silent with everyone else's sleep. I pulled up the bedroom shade and peered out into the darkness.It was now three a.m. now, and I didn't feel that I could get back to sleep. As I had other sleepless nights I watched the moon rise in the dark sky, dimming the stars. But this night in Big Bend was like no other. It gave the illusion that this little campground was the only life in the world as it slumbered innocently in the darkness, and I was the only soul awake.

I watched in awe as dawn unfolded outside my window. It began with a trillion tiny bits of light dotting the nighttime sky, forming constellations with names I never learned. The powder of sparkling stardust captured my spirit and sent it rejoicing into the stillness of the night. And then, just when my heart's song was at its fullest note, the moon entered stage right and the sparkles faded into the background, bowing to their newest performer. The golden-white luminescence lit Sportster's white spots of fur like a black light in a sixties bar and cast shadows across the campground. And yet tonight, while everyone slept, this powerful performance glided across the heavens. I was humbled by the opportunity and I silently thanked Sportster for waking me. It was a special night I would always remember.

When I opened my sleep-laden eyes, starlight had transformed into morning sunlight. My mind registered that the crisp dark air had been exchanged for warmth, promising a hot day. Reluctantly I stretched, pushing Sportster and the covers to the corner of the bed. Swinging my legs to the floor, I made the two steps to the bathroom, then, finishing, two more steps to the kitchen to push the button on the coffeemaker. As the enticing aroma filled the tiny quarters, I slid into my jeans and T-shirt, combed my hair, and performed a light make-up job.

Outside the campground was already coming to life. Motor homes were easing quietly out to the road. I remembered my ten o'clock cell phone–calling appointment with Rick and Linda and quickly checked the battery's charge, unplugged it, and slid it into my pocket. Fluffing pillows, I began to make the bed when a little cat face peered from under the covers. Sportster looked so cute and cuddly I wanted to crawl back under that cozy comforter and forget the day's plans. But time was not a luxury, so I continued fluffing and smoothing until Sportster moled his way out from under his cave of covers, hopped one hop to the kitchen sink, and waited patiently for faucet water. I doctored my coffee as Sportster had his morning water fix and we were now both ready to announce ourselves to the outside world.

I opened the shades, windows, and door to warm sunshine and fresh air. I hooked Sportster up to his retractable Harley leash threaded through the ten-pound boat anchor and plopped into my recliner with my coffee, ready to contemplate the day's activities. Sportster did his routine examination of the campsite as far as his leash would allow, threading it through the recliner's legs several times until he was tangled and unable to continue his inspection. I was forced to respond to his tiny soft "help-me" meow by rising out of my chair, crouching down, and steering him around and around the chair leg until he was released. He always acted like he didn't understand this procedure, but I'm sure that inside his feline heart, he had done this to make me prove my love.

With ten o'clock nearing, I placed Sportster inside so he could eat his breakfast and perform his bathroom duties, locked the door, and then headed down to the campsite to meet my "cell phone people." They had just come out of their rig loaded up with maps and ice chest, jackets and hats, and were loading everything into their Jeep. We exchanged cheery good mornings and quickly headed out with the directions in hand. We found the spot easily and we were all grateful they had a Jeep because the dirt road was rutted and steep in places. Rick parked at the top of the rise, and as we climbed out we were impressed by the view of the Rio Grande River threading its way through the valley below. The sky was blindingly blue and the stillness whispered. We stood, absorbing the scene, and heard faint voices from the valley below. It was a group of Mexicans waving at us from Mexico's side of the river. They were flailing their arms and yelling and pointing, and finally we made out the words, "Do you want to buy?" We looked around and noticed a small group of rocks with small items lying on them. As we approached to examine, there were a half dozen, roughly hand made little dolls of twigs, with bits of cloth for skirts. Next to them was a coffee can and on the can was written "$3.00." We surmised that we were to put the money in the can if we wanted to purchase one of these examples of indigenous Mexican culture and then, after we left, they would climb the steep quarter-mile embankment to retrieve the money. Linda, whom I had already pegged as having the charitable heart, scrounged up three one-dollar bills, first hers, then one from Rick, and the third from me. She placed them in the can, securing them with a rock that had been shrewdly placed in the can. She felt proud of her purchase and her deed. We then separated at a distance to give each other privacy as we made our phone calls.

Sandy was glad to hear from me, and had worried, even though I had told her the day before that I might not be able to call. We all felt better after talking to our loved ones and climbed back into the Jeep. Rick and Linda had a map of the park and explained that a couple of the scenic points were close, and did I want to accompany them and do some sightseeing. "Wonderful! I'd love to!" We stopped at Santa Elena Overlook and were overcome again by another fantastic view of the Rio Grande. We all imagined the Old West days of covered wagons and cowboys and Indians. And yet, at the same time, we realized that the mighty river's cut in the land separated the stark poverty of Mexican huts that had not changed since those old western days, from what now stood, in contrast across the river, affluent fifty- to sixty-thousand-dollar American motor homes that gloated of prosperity. We thought about those indigenous Mexicans, back at the cell phone stop, who just about now had reached the top of the embankment to retrieve their three dollars in the can.

We returned to the campground by noon, and I decided I had time to pack up and make a few miles before dusk. After eating a bite I unhooked, packed up, and headed out.

Chapter Five

It took over an hour to drive back through Big Bend National Park and reach the interstate. I was becoming accustomed to the silence, comfortable with the solitude. Left alone, my thoughts could wander along the well-worn paths of the past or plan and plot the days ahead. Sometimes they visited those last days with Jack, even though I had forbidden them that trip. Unheeding, they dragged out the "what ifs," the "how comes,"and the "wish I hads" and laid them all out on the table, dusting them off to examine each one. The guilt, remorse, and sadness swarmed like flies around those rotting, rancid issues. And when that happened, I grabbed the errant memories by the armful, sweeping them off the table, shooing and scolding and yanking them back from their trip.

Other times these thoughts frolicked in the solitude, flying into the unknown, visiting new possibilities and untried tasks. I let them swoop and soar until they tired of testing excitement levels and measuring instants of magnificence they had imagined.

Aloneness only set in and stole my serenity when my thoughts shoved me, with my heels dug in, to stand next to the fortunates who shared their life moments with a partner. Dodging and ducking the force of the shove, I flailed my arms and beat these thoughts back into submission, accepting reality. I was learning to discipline my thoughts, keep them in their place; then my solitude was free to create an abundance of serenity.

Right now comfortable and serene, the Wizard seemingly drifting toward the interstate, I remembered moments, not too long ago, when life was not so simple or sweet, and still other moments that were full and rich. And I was off again, reminiscing as the miles ticked by.

When Jack came home from jail the tension was taut. I was afraid I would upset him and he was afraid he would frighten me, but we kept busy trying to survive.

Because of my immaturity I had made careless and irresponsible decisions throughout my life. Those bad decisions left me suffering in depression causing my life to become more dire which in turn increased the depression. One of the seriously bad decisions I had made was taking a second out on my home. I had big ideas with little ambition. The balloon payment on the second came due and unable to meet the deadline my home went into foreclosure. Jack pushed me to make the painful decision to cut my losses and abandon ship. A customer offered a thousand dollars to take over my house loan, and I took the money and ran. With the money from our garage sale and the house bail-out money, we rented a shop in the nearby shopping center. Jack installed a tub to wash dogs, hung pegboard in the reception area, and, with his innate preciseness, made signs for the windows and the building. I notified my meager number of customers, who had been coming to my home, of my new location, and we opened our doors.

Everywhere we went Jack would stop and talk to people with dogs, praising my services. One room of the shop was designated as our private living quarters, with boxes of our leftover lives stacked to the ceiling. Our bed was the couch and next to it, my desk, which completed the bedroom-living- room-office space of the ten by ten room. A curtained window shielded the flashing neon lights at night, giving our nighttime quarters the romantic glow of poverty.

I groomed a few dogs every day with Jack, my tough tattooed Harley guy, shampooing poodles and squeezing anal glands. Evenings we bathed in the dog tub, went to AA and Alanon meetings, and came home to the darkened shopping center. We snuggled on the couch and slept with the satisfaction of an honest day's teamwork. The first month passed and we had earned enough to make the next month's rent, $400.00.

Jack's commonsense economic bailout plan was, "You have to work, work hard, and work long." Hard work can keep a business afloat, but love and attention to details will make it flourish. I had always been discontent in the grooming business because I had wanted a career that made a difference. I didn't see dog grooming as very important, but now, with Jack in the picture, I began to see through his eyes and heart. It was Jack who looked into my furry customers' brown eyes and felt their nervousness or their butt-wiggling happiness. For the first time, I began to appreciate the puppy personalities and the love and devotion of their owners. Now, when I released a dog, I felt warm inside, as pet and owner pranced and beamed with pride, going home with tail wagging and talking sweet nothings. These creatures, big and small, with their unconditional love, were members of the family. Sometimes the family was just a lonely widower whose world would have been worthless after his beloved's passing, if not for little Coco's devotion. Many times the family member was a golden retriever, playing catcher in a nine-year-old's dream of the big leagues, or a German shepherd acting guardian, sitting steadfastly by the baby carriage. And, of course, the poodles, who play the part of the clowns as they jump and jive their way through the lives of their family. Their family, who have entrusted me with their care.

There are the not-so-sweet fur balls, in the grooming world. The little poodle that, when Jack reached into the cage to retrieve it, almost bit off his finger. And I remember how, during our first week of opening, Jack, always so supportive, stood by my side as I greeted the customers entering the reception area. This day it was a young girl with her enormous Old English sheepdog. The dog bellowed out an aggressive "WOOF" that reverberated off the walls when it entered the shop. In that same instant, I glanced to my left to visualize only the shadow of my big, tattooed, supportive Harley guy, because Jack had vanished down the hall.

A plump, elderlylooking customer with silver grey hair tied in a bun came in to make an appointment for Sunday, the only day we were closed. She explained that she worked and was a Seventh Day Adventist, attending church on Saturdays. With no appointment, and muttering to herself, she left. When she finally did bring the little poodle in, he was one solid matt from the head to the tail. Not just regular matting; this dog was existing inside a plaster of paris–like cast made of hardened dog hair. After hours of careful cutting, the little guy was freed from his prison of neglect. He could not even stand because his legs were so weak. After a serious lecture, his owner did become a regular client, and the dog became a happy, pampered pet.

Some stories were not happy endings. A young girl brought in a shitzu. The girl had been living with her dad after he had divorced her mother. She was in town visiting her mother, and discovered the family pet matted and full of fleas. Feeling sorry for the dog, she explained that she had persuaded her mom to let her take it in to be groomed. I shaved the flea-infested dog and gave it a bath. After the bath, as I was finishing up the grooming, the dog collapsed. "I think this dog just died," I informed Ellen, my employee as I examined the limp body on my table. Then, slowly, the little dog lifted his head and looked sadly at me. "Call the customer and tell her she needs to get her dog to the vet *now!*"

Ellen left the room to make the call and returned with her hand covering the receiver. "She says she can't do it right now because she has painting contractors at her house."

"Did you tell her the dog is gravely ill?"

"Yes, I did." I couldn't believe what I was hearing!

"Then ask her if she will pay the bill if I take it to the vet."

"She said yes." Driving to the vet's office two blocks away, I had time to surmise that the dog was probably anemic from the flea infestation, and explained my theory when I arrived. Later that day the vet called to confirm my diagnosis, explaining he would keep the dog overnight and give it transfusions. It died during the night.

When the woman came to reimburse me for the vet bill, she blamed the dog's condition on her neighbor who had sprayed his yard for fleas, forcing them to evacuate to her yard.

A fourteen-year-old Maltese was a regular at the shop but this day was not doing well. I called the owner to inform her and she understandingly said she would be right down. She came quickly but the dog expired before she arrived. "Don't you worry about it, honey," she reassured me as I wiped the tears from my eyes. "She was old and she had a good life. I am so sorry to put you through this." She sent *us* flowers the next day.

And finally there was the cocker spaniel that bit me in the face, tearing my lip. The dog had been upset over the grooming process, and in my experience I knew I should have put the dog back in a cage to calm down. But I was in a hurry that day, and when I tried to pick up the spaniel to comfort him, he lunged for my face, ripping my lip. I had Jack drive me to the hospital and, as I walked into the ER with a bloody towel to my mouth, Jack nervously but earnestly explained to the admitting nurse that I had been bitten by a dog. He later explained that it was the first time he had accompanied a female to an emergency room who hadn't had injuries inflicted by him. "I didn't know how to act. I didn't have to feel guilty," he admitted.

My lip with nine stitches head and Jack continued as the months passed to lecture on the merits of a successful business: Never turn a customer away. That was his premise and it became mine. We were aware and appreciated that each patron was paying our meager bills and was responsible for the growth of our little savings account. But my childish spoiled attitude didn't surrender easily, and convinced me that I was chained to the grooming table—I couldn't help feeling sorry for myself that there would be no more fun in my life. But I worked anyway. As the money began to accumulate, I became aware of the rewards of hard work. It was wonderful.

Because of Jack's alcoholism he'd applied for disability, and his first check had arrived. He didn't want to add it to the pot. This money, he claimed, was like an inheritance, not to be shared. I burst into a rage. I felt hurt and used. What about all this togetherness? I was doing all the work and paying the bills. It did not seem fair, I argued. Finally he conceded. With his check we made a down payment on a small trailer in an old mobile home park. We moved out of the shop into our little empire that boasted a single bed and a real bathtub.

Our togetherness continued as we ate together, worked together, and slept together. But I was used to a lifetime of freedom from the responsibilities of a business that my mother had managed, and independence from any kind of real relationship. I pranced and side-stepped, wanting to run from it all. Jack told me how to do my grooming; the best way to clean our little home, and, he didn't like the way I pulled weeds. I wanted to go out with friends; he said no. "You are married now. You don't need to be out running around anymore." I resented him and felt confined. But I learned routine. I learned to accomplish a good day's work by using the evening to relax and rejuvenate for the next day. The money I was making made up for the lack of fun with my friends.

His control angered and smothered me, but his devotion and his common sense about living became a part of me. So the months passed and I worked, suffered his restraints, and worked more. But I couldn't work all the time, and coming home to our little nest of confinement soon became unbearable. I felt suffocated and the fear of that night a year ago still haunted me. I was sure we were past the violence but I did not have the courage to test it. I told Jack I wanted a divorce. I expected the anger and arguments to arise but

I was relieved and surprised that we had built up enough respect for each other during that year that we honored each other's wishes. When he reacted maturely to the separation, my respect for him grew. The no-nonsense divorce was quick and without animosity. I kept the business and took up residence at the shop, while Jack remained in the little trailer with his disability checks.

Now, thanks to Jack, I had learned routine and good work habits. I worked and slept and worked and slept. I did attend my Al-Anon meetings regularly, learning the rules of life, love, and tolerance. Slowly I began to breathe easier, without Jack's constant control issues. We began talking on the phone and went on dates. Jack respected my need for space and, although I missed him terribly, I knew we needed to go slowly to build a healthy relationship. I knew I was not yet strong enough to break the chains of his controlling personality.

I acquired a German shepherd puppy after the divorce and began obedience and protection training with her. She was a scrawny puppy that the breeder had nursed back to life from a case of parvo. Her littermates would have nothing to do with her, so, with both of us needing a friend, we bonded. She was with me constantly. My sister suggested the name Masada, the name of a plateau in Israel where the Jews battled the Romans until they could fight no longer, and, instead of surrendering, they committed suicide. The name suited her and her purpose. She was going to give me courage to deal with Jack. I was thrilled, andas her confidence grew during training, so did mine. Just one word, and she became alert, ready to defend. No one would intimidate me again. I would become the intimidator. She had refined lines in her black face and her tan legs showed a shadow of redness. Still considered a puppy at six months, her huge ears flopped comically when she romped and played, tripping over her huge paws. She didn't care when I went out and with whom I had been. She was just happy I was home. This was a relationship I could handle, and it was all I had going for me. I couldn't wait to see Jack and demonstrate my new bodyguard.

But Jack was not one to be outdone. Shortly after meeting Masada and going to a few training sessions with me, he met a man who was selling all his possessions and moving onto a houseboat. The man could not keep his German shepherd, Storm, which had been protection-trained and imported from Germany. Jack and I drove out to see the dog, and the man offered to put the shepherd through its paces. We both declined, worried that if we saw what the dog was capable of, we would be afraid of him.

We brought Storm back with us and he was the sweetest dog. He would lay his head on my knee, or Jack's and soak up affection for hours if we were so inclined to give it.

"This is no protection dog." Jack was disappointed.

Storm would lie on the concrete coolness of the attached screened-in patio in the afternoons. About a week later, a young man, soliciting yard work in the trailer park by slipping flyers into the doors of the mobile homes, approached the patio's screen door. Storm, who was sound asleep on the floor, twitched his ears and feet as if he was dreaming of frolicking in clover with a young lady friend. The innocent solicitor reached to slip the flyer into the screen door and, in one beat of his heart, saw that sweet loving dog transformed into a raging, roaring, vicious bear, rearing on his back legs and pounding the thin screen door with his front paws in an attempt to reach the pale, wide-eyed stranger. His flyers went flying into the vacuum of air where he had once stood, because by the young man's second heartbeat, he was already a hundred yards down the street.

"I guess he *is* protection trained." Jack was as startled as the escaping stranger but a smile of pride slowly spread across his face.

Our time was now spent going to the training grounds with Storm and Masada, fine-tuning their protection skills. We had an evil delight in packing the dogs into the back of the station wagon and parking in the Alano Club parking lot near the club's entrance. As the poor recovering AA and Al-Anon members approached the entrance, passing the station wagon with the windows cracked open, they would begin to admire the beautiful shepherds lying lazily in the back. As they neared with oohs and ahhs, Storm would wait until they were just inches from the car, and then morph into this Cujo monster of their worst nightmares, with teeth bared and hair on end. Masada would provide backup. Jack and I would watch the performance from a distance. No one said we were emotionally healthy.

A mobile home next door to Jack's became available, and I decided that I could live next door to him, just not with him. After I purchased it, Jack put my name on the mailbox. Now his mailbox and mine had the same name, "J. Howard," but under my name he wrote, "Hers" and under his name, "His." He spent most of his time at my place and still tried to run my life. He explained, "If you would wash the car or scrub the floor this way, you would not be overworking yourself." He still tried to run my life but because most of his suggestions were valid, I learned his meticulous ways. And most importantly, I learned to stand up for myself. Jack had always explained to people that when he met me, "She was this little butterfly that just flitted around and was nice to everyone. Then she met me. Now she packs a thirty-eight, drives a four by four truck, and has a German shepherd attack dog."

I remember how the thirty-eight came into my possession. Masada would go to work every day with me. She spent most of her time sleeping under my grooming table, but would come out to be admired by the customers and get pats on the head. If you sang "God Bless America" or "Happy Birthday," she would sing along in a howling accompaniment, and with a little encouragement she would say, "I love you," in her own doggie dialect. The customers always enjoyed her performances. I also gave obedience classes in the evenings and she was the excellent example of what the efforts of training could produce. All the human students wanted their pets to aspire to Masada's level, although the dog students weren't always so impressed. She became a favorite of the customers, who were never aware of her protection capabilities. I often wondered if something happened for real, and not on the training grounds, how she would react.

To my regret, the day came when my wondering ceased. I remember it had been just another normal day at work, the day before Thanksgiving, in fact. My three employees and I had been busy all morning, and we were getting ready to take a lunch break. Ellen, my manager had disappeared down the hall to put the toy poodle she had just finished grooming in a cage. Sheri, Kelly and I gathered in the break room sharing a pizza that had just been delivered.

He had burst into the space from nowhere, while pushing Ellen in front of him. She still clutched the little poodle in her trembling arms as his gun hand shoved her into the room's center. We all looked up in surprise from eating our pizza, then fear must have registered on our faces as we saw the gun. But only he could have seen our fear, as he pointed the twenty-two caliber, because all eyes were on him. He was short and dark-complexioned. Later we all had different descriptions. I thought he was Iranian, two of the girls thought he was black, and the true description ended up being Puerto Rican.

From under my grooming table, Masada came barreling forward.

"Call off the dog or I will shoot him," his voice boomed in the small room, and the crack of the pistol exploded before any words came out of my mouth. My heart broke and rage filled my mind, but I had to stay, frozen in place.

"Now give me the money or you're next." The gun and those small black eyes were aimed directly at me. Masada collapsed under my table. I scrambled for the few dollars in my pocket and, shakily handed it over.

"Now give me the keys to that car." He pointed to a car parked outside by the window.

"That car doesn't belong to any of us. It belongs to the shop next door." Kelly was denying ownership of her own car. What was she doing?

"Then give me the keys to the truck parked out front." He became more agitated.

Jack and I had just bought the brand new little Dodge Ram. It had only sixty miles on it. We had argued that morning. He had wanted me to take the old car and I had whined successfully, wanting to take the new truck.

I rummaged frantically for the keys. This was not the time to lose my keys in the abyss of my purse. What seemed like forever finally passed, and my keys appeared. The robber snatched them and was gone so fast, I wondered if the last terrifying minutes of my life had occurred at all. I ordered the girls to call 911, and went to check on Masada. She was breathing but trembling uncontrollably as she went into shock. I quickly gave the police the truck's description, called Jack, and we scooped Masada into the car of denied ownership.

The veterinarian's office was closed for lunch hour, so we went to the side door and hammered frantically until someone answered. They assured us they would take her into surgery immediately, and I rushed back to the shop to talk to the police. They had already captured the guy. When they had chased him, he had sideswiped two cars and run into a business named "Brake City." The new little truck's short life was over. It was totaled. It was a thrilling story in the paper the next day that covered the police chase and the shooting of the dog.

Jack arrived at the shop and I collapsed into his arms. Minutes passed as I absorbed his strength and as, he too, shook with anger and his fear for me. The truck was incidental compared to what could have happened.

Masada's doggie angel had watched over her. The bullet had hit her large canine tooth and went no further. The vet explained that the canine teeth, the fangs, are one of the strongest parts of the body. They only had to remove bullet fragments from her gums. She was going to be fine. We found the bullet on the grooming room floor.

Jack had a friend in AA, named Rick, who could never stay sober. His folks were customers of mine. Rick was only twenty and in and out of jail all the time. Two days after the robbery, I received a phone call from Rick.

"Do you know where I am?" he questioned.

"No."

"I am in jail and I just wanted you to know we took care of that guy for you. We had a blanket party for him last night and told him, "You shot the wrong dog, dude.""

Jails have their own justice and it is swift. The worst inmates, guilty of the most heinous crimes, will defend an animal or child against injustice. That is why child abusers are usually separated from the general population for their own safety. A blanket party occurs after an inmate falls asleep. The inmates doling out their justice quickly wrap the offender in a blanket and then they all beat him to within an inch of his life, sometimes further, if it gets out of control. The rage I felt eased a little after Rick's phone call. At the lineup, our perp's face was wrapped in bandages. "What happened to him?" I asked innocently.

Jack had always said that if I owned a business. I should have a gun.

"Oh, I could never shoot anyone." After the robbery, I couldn't get to the gun store fast enough. I purchased a thirty-eight revolver. I spent time at the shooting range to get comfortable with it even though as a child, my father had taken my sister and me target-practicing at the river many times: I was not the shrinking violet. I carried my thirty-eight everywhere for over a year. I packed it in my purse or my pocket. I wanted to shoot someone. I was mad as hell. I realized I was glad the robbery had happened because I learned to be more aware of people around me, taking notice of who was approaching my car or my person. No longer was I that little butterfly flitting around thinking everything was wonderful. Bad things can happen to nice people.

The robbery had brought Jack and me even closer—maybe because of his fear of almost losing me, or perhaps he was just afraid of my gun. He seemed to treat me with more respect, and I cherished the nights following the robbery, when he held me with quiet understanding. When I awoke from nightmares and cried, his arms wrapped me in safety. Across from our trailer park were wide-open spaces of sagebrush, boulders, and grassy hills. We would take long walks so far back into the hills with Masada and Storm that it seemed as if we were the only ones in the world. We would release the dogs and sit in the lush green grass watching them, yipping like coyotes, in their own heaven as they chased rabbits they would never catch. They would finally drop to the ground next to us, with their tongues hanging out and tails wagging, collapsing in total exhaustion.

Sunday mornings were grocery-shopping days. The store opened at seven a.m., so at six a m. we would arrive at our favorite mom-and-pop restaurant for breakfast. It was a romantic interlude after a week of working and the daily chores of living. Jack would always banter with the waitress and we would discuss the past week's events and plans and hopes for the coming one. We had become comfortable with each other's habits, desires, and dislikes, and were becoming the proverbial old married couple. The separateness of the divorce and living quarters sealed our security. When an unsolvable argument ensued, we would each retreat to our separate corners in our respective mobile homes, as if a bell clanged the end of a round. We took rounds of togetherness and then retreated when differences dashed blows to our confidences.

Jack bought a touring bike and we joined a motorcycle club. He eagerly explained to me that the members were just ordinary working people. We went on monthly rides and although I enjoyed the rides, Jack had difficulty with some of the club members' personalities. He was trying to recreate the drunken camaraderie of his days in the Hell's Angels and these people were *not* the Hell's Angels. They were sober everyday working stiffs. One ride took us through a small community twenty miles from our trailer park. It was early fall, with the trees in full color and an aroma of chimney smoke hanging in the damp morning fog. The crisp smoke-scented air filled me with nostalgia for childhood, when I would sit by a warm fire watching snowflakes drift past the window.

Intrigued one day by a for-sale sign on a small house with a window looking out to the hills, on a whim we called the realtor and went to see the little cabin. The living, dining, and kitchen area had a warm glow from the homey knotty pine that lined the walls. Filling the living room was a massive brick fireplace next to a window of equal size that opened to the beautiful hills and sunsets. It had only two bedrooms, one so small that Jack claimed it as his because it reminded him of a jail cell. Thirty days later we were the proud but surprised owners of this little cabin. Jack, who had never been able to hold on to anything in his life, now had a home and a woman to call his own. Five years had sped by almost unnoticed. My business had been doing well enough for me to qualify for the loan. The day we closed escrow, we sat in amazement on the front porch, enraptured by the quietness of this country setting, listening to a fly buzzing and the wind rustling the dried grasses of autumn, as a fiery sun sank below the hills. With gratitude and pride, we became aware that the pages of our lives had turned into chapters.

So now, I was driving this rain-soaked highway, at this time in my life without my Jack. But he was there, ingrained in every ounce of my being. I was only here on the road because this special man had stumbled into my life, picked me up, poked here, and prodded there, until I was finished. He was the wind beneath my wings, albeit a gale at times. And though to the outside world, it always appeared that Jack, who had come from such a miserable life, was the lucky one to have such a woman as me, it really was I who was the blessed one. Everything we had done together beat anything I had done alone. I could go on now, the finished product, polished in compassion, caring, and tolerance, to experience what the rest of life has in store for me, the next defining moment.

Chapter Six

As I moved on down the road toward the inter-state, I noticed that the rain had lessened to a mist, and I couldn't imagine the possibility of any more defining moments in my life: with the exception of Jack not being here, my life seemed blessed and full.

Back on the interstate, leaving Big Bend to my memory, I headed for San Antonio, but first two places intrigued me: The Davey Crockett Monument and The Caverns of Sonora.

The Davey Crockett monument was unveiled in 1913. and features a bonneted pioneer woman standing on a pedestal, her hand forever shading her eyes as she looked to the west, eternally won-dering when her husband was coming home. The statue was placed over the gravesite of Elizabeth Patton Crockett, the wife of Davey Crockett, the former U.S. congressman from Tennessee. I remem-ber Davey Crockett and the ballad I sang as a kid. Davey Davey Crocket, king of the wild frontier who killed him a 'bar' when he was only three. He fought in 'many a war' and ' made himself a legend forever more' Davey Crocket, the man ' who knew no fear'. He went to congress and served a spell, fixin up the laws and even 'patched up the crack in the liberty bell.'

History goes on to report that Davey's "politikin' was done" when his constituents did not re-elect him. At one time he had called Texas the "garden spot of the world," so he announced to his constituents,, "Since you have chosen a timber toe to succeed me, you may all go to hell and I will go to Texas." And so he did. Davey was killed in the battle at the Alamo swinging his rifle, "Old Betsy." in 1836. Seventeen years later, his wife Elizabeth, still living in Tennessee, received payment from Texas for her husband's services,1,280 acres in north Texas, but the Comanches roamed the area and saw the land as theirs. It wasn't until eight years after Texas became a state, that Mrs. Crockett left Tennessee with her two grown children, Robert and Matilda, to claim her land. After the surveyor's fee, she ended up with 640 acres near Rucker's Creek, about six miles from Granbury. Elizabeth lived there in her husband's beloved land of Texas until January 31, 1860. at age 74, she died during a morning walk. She still wore the widow's black that she had worn since first hearing of her husband's death in 1836. The monument in Acton is a state historic site and the smallest state park in Texas.

My next stop was the Caverns of Sonora, which were beautiful in their own right. I decided to spend the night at the campground on the Mayfield Ranch, the cavern's owners. By the time I toured the caverns and settled in at my campsite, it was sundown and another day had wound down. As I lay in bed that night, I reviewed my trip's progress. It was my sixth night on the road and not a glitch. I was amazed and timidly swelled with pride in the privacy of darkness. Recalling that first night in Quartzite, I check my bleeding heart and realized, although it was still raw from mourning, it beat a little more confidently with the faint hope that it would go on. And in the meantime, I was going to make it! Ihad gone over thirteen hundred miles! One day at a time, one hour at a time, and one mile at a time. But my heart was a strange machine and, just after it pumped confidently, it skipped a beat as Jack Incarnate, who can always ruin a victorious moment, reminded me we were only halfway, and anything can happen. Dejectedly I agreed with him, rolling away from my window, curling into a ball. I hugged my pillow and dozed off into restless slumber.

I leaned into him, my face against his chest, as his arms wrapped me in what was the most intimate embrace of all time. After twenty-five years, his touch still sent me into shivers of weakness. Slowly, his hands slid down my back, feather-light over the slight of my hips, and pressed me to him. There were no words for this intimate moment. His body felt like the universe to me as I floated and glowed in his presence, and once again, the entire world was mine.

I awoke remembering the dream, and just the memory sent my spirit soaring. I wanted to go back into the dream and never return, but the starkness of daylight and reality was already blinding my eyes as I peered from under the covers. A new day had begun.

I dressed quickly and primped lightly while the coffee perked and Sportster crunched his breakfast and pushed litter around in his bathroom. Seven days on the road and I am only halfway to my destination. I decided I should cut down on the sightseeing if I am going to reach my destination by Thanksgiving.

I was cruising down the interstate just as the sun tried to appear in the Texan heavens. The weather was stormy and overcast. As the hours clicked by, patches of sunshine changed to patches of rain-soaked clouds offering down an easy shower. It would be romantic to take a hand-in-hand stroll through this hill country. I recalled the rainy afternoons with Jack when we took the dogs running in the hills. We would trail behind, wrapped in our own warmth and like two admiring parents, watching our "children" having the time of their lives, as we would sneak sweet nothings after catching raindrops on our tongues.

I made good time, stopping only for gas, leg stretching, and potty breaks. I made Houston by late afternoon, just in time for rush hour. My intention was to get though to the other side of the city before nightfall. It was the peak of the afternoon, about three, when I noticed that the skies were no longer displaying heaven-blues and cotton-whites as they had an hour ago. I was now in the midst of Houston's commuter traffic and the skies were ominous black with swirls of gray. Tornado clouds. I switched the radio to a local station and listened, dreading what I knew was the forecast: tornado warnings. The traffic was only inching along. Why don't these people get moving? I pictured the motor home in a scene from *The Wizard of Oz*, twisting up through the dark skies, never to be seen again, with me, like a red flag flapping in the black wind, hanging on by my fingernails to the back bumper with the sticker that says "Home is where you park it." *"I told you we should never have come on this trip!! It is too far!! We are going to die! How could I have ever let you talk me into this!! Every time I should have known better than to listen to you and what do I do? I do it any way!!* If I could just get out of this traffic jam, I could get out of town and leave the bad weather behind me, and Jack Incarnate would shut up. He was making me cry now. The tears were rolling down my cheeks as I blinked to make clear the ominous scene in front of me. I said a few prayers and then I said a few more. What seemed endless, was about an hour, before I got through Houston, leaving the tornado warning behind me, so I thought.

Leaving Houston, I was really shaken by my experience. What seemed like a near miss settled like a dark cloud in the back of my mind. I couldn't let it go. Jack Incarnate was still grumbling. I was still gripping the steering wheel, my fingers aching, when I crossed the state line into Louisiana. Almost immediately my rig started shaking, banging, bumping. What was this? Potholes? A stretch of bad road, literally. I slowed down to fifty but I still feared the rig would shatter into pieces. Forty miles an hour seemed almost bearable, although cars and semis were whizzing past me, giving me dirty looks. Just when the road would smooth out and

I would pick up speed, there would be another patch of potholes that would almost shake the cabinet doors loose. I gave up trying to make time; I poked along at forty miles an hour. Finally, stressed and bone-tired, I pulled into a Love's truck stop in Lake Charles, still wanting to cry. I had had enough adventure for one day. I climbed out and slowly stretched out my arms, my back, even my fingers that felt like lead, and walked inside. I bought a cup of coffee to go and went back to my rig. A little Chinook motor home had parked next to me, although I didn't see its occupants. I didn't care anyway. I didn't feel sociable. Inside my cave, I pulled out one of my little squares from the freezer, nuked it in the microwave, and ate it without noticing or caring what it was. I then called my friend Vickie in Florida and told her of my horrible day. She told me months later, after my trip was over and I was home safe and sound, that she had relayed the story of my horrid day to her husband, whom I had not met yet and who didn't know what kind of determined person I can be. He had asked her, "So is she turning around and going home?" My friend only smiled at him that night and said, "No." I finished the rest of my calls, feeling a little better after dumping my bad day on the rest of my concerned friends, got into my pajamas, and crawled into bed.

I slept like a tired puppy. It was midnight when I awoke to the sound of rain crashing against the doors, the windows, and the roof, like an intruder trying to break down my thin walls of protection.

The entire motor home was swaying severely. I got up and looked out into the dimly lit parking lot. Sheets of water, blown horizontal by the fierce wind, had an eerie gray glow. The wind was screaming, a howling sound like some abandoned dog aching over its loss. I was terrified. I have never seen a storm so severe since I was a child in Illinois. I got dressed. If I was going to be blown away, I didn't want to be in my pj's. The vengeance of the storm lasted a lifetime, thirty minutes. The rain receded to just a heavy downpour. I finally thought of turning on the radio, just in time to catch a news report of a tornado touching down in Lake Charles. I was so glad I didn't know it was a tornado when it was happening. I know I would have died from the fear. And I had thought I had had a bad day when I went to bed. Not so. *Now* I've had a bad day!! I lay in bed fully dressed and, waiting for daylight, listened to the now-gentle lull of the rain. I wasn't in a contemplative mood—I just wanted to get some form of rest, get on the road, and leave this day far behind me.

I missed Jack terribly. I was so alone, I ached. Suddenly the burdens of this trip weighed almost unbearably on me. I felt sorry for myself. What do I do, now that I'm all alone? Our marriage was difficult at times but when the chips were down we always rallied together. We were a great team. Jack was always there to watch my back. Anyone and everyone could forsake me, but he was my companion, my friend, and my soul mate, forever by my side. And then, quietly as the rain pattered a magical tune on the roof, I felt his presence.

People would say I was just imagining things, but Jack was there in the early morning dimness. I felt so warm, so calm, so loved.

I had felt his presence at other times. A week to the day after his passing, I was coming home from work and passed my neighbor, Loretta, who was digging in her yard. Feeling really sad and wondering how I would make it through one more hour, I stopped. She came up and gave me a long hug as I cried.

"Oh Judy, don't feel bad dear. Jack told me you were the best thing that ever happened to him," she whispered into my ear as she embraced me. At that moment I heard, not her voice, but Jack's. It was so clear I turned my head, thinking he must be standing there, and of course he wasn't there, but a serenity and warmth washed over me. I felt that same calmness now in the early morning light and I knew everything was going to be fine. I dozed off for a couple of hours of much needed rest.

Chapter Seven

Morning came with bright sunshine piercing through the storm clouds and warming the steaming asphalt of the parking lot. I crawled out of bed still fully dressed, mentally and physically ready for this new day. I fixed a cup of instant coffee, planted myself in the driver's seat, and, ready for new adventures, eased out of the truck stop onto the I-10.

The road and its potholes had not improved overnight so I crept along at fifty-five miles per hour. I noticed several trees uprooted as proof of the power of last night's storm. I was feeling quite lucky that all I had lost was a good night's sleep.

It was daybreak and I was anxious to leave this part of the country behind. I later learned that Lake Charles was located on a plain thirty miles from the Gulf and had a strong Cajun culture. Fresh-water marshes and scenic rivers lured the outdoor recreationists. while casinos lured the gamblers: L'Auberge du Lac Resort and Casino being the tallest structure between Houston and Baton Rouge, at twenty-six stories. The city hosted one of the largest celebrations in Louisiana, a twelve-day festival called Contraband Days with an attendance of over 200,000. It honored the legend of a pirate named Jean Lafitte who, with his band of men, frequented the area's waterways. Legend had it that Lafitte buried his contraband somewhere in the city's vicinity. Every year the festivities were kicked off by a pirate ship bombardment to "take control of the city" at the seawall. A gang of rowdy and unruly buccaneers, led by "Jean Lafitte." overran the blazing cannons of the local militia and raised their "Jolly Roger" flag, capturing the mayor. With swords drawn they made the mayor walk the plank into the swirling waters of the lake. It sounded like a fun-filled twelve days and made me want to return, but what was this ahead of me? The sign announced the Calcasieu River High Bridge. I swallowed hard as I eased onto the span that was crossing the river. It was 850 feet long and the same height as the L'Auberge Du Lac Casino, twenty-six stories, but it carried me up, over, and across the river before I could panic. In no time at all I was cruising on solid ground, leaving Lake Charles behind.

Baton Rouge, the capital of Louisiana, was fast approaching. It was located on the Mississippi River and upstream from the Istrouma Bluff. It was the first bluff upriver from the delta and was a natural barrier, protecting the city from flooding and hurricanes. The city also was home to the Magnolia Mound Plantation, its architecture influenced by the early settlers from France and the West Indies, and illustrating the lifestyle of the French Creoles who formed the fascinating culture that still influenced Southern Louisiana. All was well until I saw another bridge ahead, and Jack Incarnate began humming the music from the movie *Jaws*: "*Dah dum. Dah Dum. Dah Dum.*"

Atchafalya Basin Bridge in Baton Rouge was really two parallel bridges that spanned the Atchafalya Swamp, the nation's largest swamp. It was a combination of wetlands and river delta as the Mississippi River and the Gulf of Mexico converge. Bald cypress, bayous, and marshes make their home here. I approached the too-narrow bridge that led me over not just water, but swamp water, as far as I could see. The Calcasieu River High Bridge was scary enough, but it spanned the Mississippi River. I was raised by the Mississippi River. I've swum in the muddy Mississippi. But this! All I saw was dark murkiness when I dared a look as I proceeded onto the bridge. I tightened my already firm grip on the wheel. I was afraid to look into the water because the steering wheel tended to follow the direction of my gaze. If I looked too long I would surely drive right into that dark, smelly, murky lagoon slithering with snakes and alligators. I could already feel the steely cold water lapping on my face as, kicking and flailing, I treaded water frantically. The dark green bumpy eyes of a creature sliding nearer and nearer. Snap!! I felt excruciating pain in my leg from the alligator's powerful jaws!! Oh no, it was just a cramp in my leg that pulled me back to the reality of crossing this endless swamp full of creepy, crawly creatures on this way-too-narrow two-lane bridge. How long *was* this bridge? I was afraid to look down at the odometer. My fingers ached, and my shoulders and neck screamed for relief from the tension. I didn't know how I could keep on driving. I couldn't turn around. There was nowhere to stop. It was just as well, because if I stopped I knew I would not have it in me to start up again. I would be frozen with fear. So I kept driving. How long was this bridge? For the first time on this trip, Jack Incarnate was quiet. I dared to glance over at him. He was passed out, his head leaning on the cool window. Even Sportster was crouched on the dash, keeping a vigilant green eye on the churning waters.

My brain screamed, my heart thundered, and my palms sweated. God, I hoped my grip on the wheel didn't slip. The traffic was moving at a quick clip. No time to dally. No time to absorb the mysterious beauty of the dark blue-black watercolors. The reeds of bright green rising erect above the water level hid the secret creatures lurking in its forest. A thought niggled behind my fear that an airboat would get me up close to this mystical world. I would like to do that. But now the job was to just make it across this endless bridge. *How long was this bridge?* Then . . . I saw land! It was still far ahead but I was going to make it. I looked at the odometer. Eighteen miles. The Atchafalya Basin Bridge was eighteen miles long!

Not again! And even longer! I had traveled just under one hundred miles and just when I was breathing easy again, I was confronted with The

Twin Spans, as they are locally called. They cross the eastern end of Lake Pontchatrain in southern Louisiana from New Orleans to Slidell. spanning twenty-three miles. Twenty- three miles!

All I saw as the land ended was a double rib-bon of road floating on beautiful blue-green water. The black ribbons stretched endlessly into the unknown. There was no distant shore in sight. Lake Pontchartrain was green-clean, not slime-swampy like Atchafalaya Basin. And although the water seemed pristine, one hazardous mistake, one deadly wrong turn of the wheel and all that was mine would plunge through the thin railing into this bottomless lake with a name I couldn't pronounce. I couldn't breathe as my mind saw my bloody fingertips scraping the window's glass, struggling to claw my way out of my imaginary watery grave while Sportster's big green eyes stared, pleading, as his little mouth gasped for air. The driver's door was sealed like a closed coffin by the pressure of the dark cold waters. Everything was sinking: my beloved home, my bed, my clothes, my Tupperware containers of food, sink-ing into the blackened bottom of the lake. And Jack Incarnate's words echoing in the deep, *"I told you so! I told you so! But you had to go!"* I grasped at the emptiness and flailed through the terrifying thoughts that pressurized my beating heart until I couldn't breathe. Suddenly, the rush-ing sound of air being sucked into my starving lungs crashed into the dead silence of the moment. That moment was twenty-three miles long. I must have been holding my breath for twenty-three miles.

I had just crossed the longest bridge in the world and lived to tell about it!

God get me out of this part of the country! I glanced at Jack Incarnate and he was coming around. *"I don't feel so good. I want to go home. I wish I had never came. Ooooh, can we pull over?!"* He still had his head against the coolness of the window. There weren't any turnouts and I just wanted to keep going, to get past this marshy, swampy, snaky, alligator-infested area as fast as I could. But this was the South. I neared Mobile, Alabama: how many states had I conquered? I didn't have time to add them up and, at this point, I was not impressed with myself. I just wanted to finish this job I had started. I had gone too far to quit, and the stuff I'm made of wouldn't let me, anyway.

And now what? A tunnel! I was in the confines of the George Wallace Tunnel and out the other end just as Jack Incarnate screamed, *"Is this tunnel high enough? Are we going to clear it? Don't get so close to the sides! God, it's dark in here! Are your lights on? I can't see!"* Just as the relief of bright sunlight brightened my dark mood, I gasped in disbelief. *Another bridge!* The Jubilee Parkway, the sign announced. And here we go again. Jack Incarnate's face became red with anger. *"Well, son of a bitch! This is not fucking fun anymore! I can't believe you! What could you have possibly thought, taking a trip like this? I want you to turn around now and go home. I have had enough!"* At least there were two lanes, and I crossed Mobile Bay quickly, as the bridge was a mere seven miles long. I learned later that the name Jubilee was used for a natural phenomenon that occurs sporadically a couple times a year on the shores of Mobile Bay. During a "Jubilee," many species of crab and shrimp, as well as flounder and eels, would leave deep waters and swarm in large numbers and high density into specific, shallower areas of the bay. A Jubilee was a celebrated event in Mobile, attracting large crowds drawn by the promise of abundant and easy-to-catch seafood.

There was no Jubilee now. and I was not jubilant. I couldn't wait to leave Mobile and this part of the South far behind me as I crossed the Florida state line. I had made it to Florida! I quickly passed through Pensacola, the city of five flags. The flags fly for the various countries that have occupied the city: Spain, France, Great Britain, the Confederate US, and the United States. It was home of the "Blue Angels" and was called the canoe capital of Florida because of the pure sand bottom of the Blackwater River. Other nicknames were "The world's whitest beaches," because of the white sand along the panhandle; "The Cradle of Naval Aviation," for the National Museum of Naval Aviation; "Redneck Riviera," and "The Red Snapper Capital of the World."

And next came Panama City, whose beaches were rated second-best in the country. The white sands were from quartz crystals that were bleached, ground, and polished as they were washed down from the Appalachian mountains centuries ago. The city also was home to the

bottlenose dolphins at Shell Island, and lured kay-
akers and canoeists along its twenty-two miles
of curving creek at Econfina Creek Canoe Trail.
This was just another place to come back to and
experience its many wonders.

By the time I reached Tallahassee, I was
exhausted and too tired to find a campground.

The rest stop was also a visitor center. I pulled
in, worn out and weary I climbed out to stretch
my aching muscles. It was a beautiful respite from
the interstate. Huge cypress dripping with moss
proved I was in Florida. Of course the parking lot
was asphalt, but that ended the resemblance to
other rest stops. Lush green lawns framed curving
walkways of brick. The paths meandered through
this plantation-like setting, leading to the visitor's
center that was a replica of a Victorian estate. I
strolled along, stretching my stiff legs and enjoying
the flowerbeds that embraced the brick paths.
Occasionally a wrought-iron bench invited me to
sit and soak up the essence of this southern place.

I didn't stop but continued on to the visitors'
center. Weary travelers who also had discovered
the magic of this place were entering and exit-
ing through a big oak door with stained glass.
Their casualness defied the fact that they faced
many more stressful miles of driving to their various
adventures. The beauty and peace of this place
definitely calmed the tired traveler. As I pulled
open the big oak door, my senses were stirred with
the aroma of freshly brewed coffee, but it was
the scene before me that caused me to pause in
awe. I had stepped into the parlor of a southern

plantation. The volunteers were dressed in elegant gowns of that grand era. There were the usual racks of brochures, but they weredisguised in a setting of Victorian furniture and tapestry.

Amazed at the transformation of an ordinary rest stop, I was swept back into a magical time when everything was slower and grander. One of the volunteers offered a cup of that magnificent smelling coffee that I sipped as I slowly browsed the museum-like atmosphere. Finally, I dropped money into the donation box and headed back outside and back to the Wizard. I noticed signs that warned of twenty-four-hour security patrols and surveillance cameras that made me feel safe. It was dusk and I planned to spend the night but I was nervous because most rest stops warned of no overnight parking, although many travelers, and nearly all truckers, made it a common practice. I was tired and decided that if security came knocking on my door in the middle of the night, then I would have to move on.

As I approached my rig, a woman was coming out of her motor home that was parked beside me. She asked if I had seen which way her husband had walked. I point to the path I had seen him meander down and then I pointed to Jack Incarnate, still sitting in the passenger seat

"See my guy? He never wanders off!"

She looked up and when it registered that he was just a doll, she laughed.

"That's what I need!"

"He never gives me any trouble," I joked, as she took off in search of her misplaced husband, her chuckling fading into the dusk as she headed down the path.

Back inside, I sighed a long, long sigh. What a day this had been! I wanted to cry, I was so tired, and I collapsed onto the couch. And wouldn't you know? Who came to my rescue? Sportster did his casual yoga-like stretch on the dash and slowly made his way to the floor and onto my lap. Purring his loud song called "I love only you" and placing his soft paws on my neck, he massaged my bruised and battered travel muscles. I never considered that he was selfishly "making muffins" because it soothes him; I was a cat owner now and told myself he was comforting me. And he was. I didn't feel so alone as I ran my fingers through his soft warmness. As I sat there, I picked up my maps and calculations and, scanning over them, realized that tomorrow I will arrive at my destination. Tomorrow was Thanksgiving Day. Too tired to get really excited, I began making my calls. First to my sister, who said she couldn't believe I was almost there. I told her about my day and the bridges and she made a note of the rest stop. Wearily, I ended the call. And then Vickie. I told her I wasn't sure what time I would arrive but it should be before five. I told her not to hold dinner, that just being there was enough for me and, anyway, I loved leftovers. The conversation picked me up as reality set in that tomorrow, I not only would I have accomplished a great feat, but I won't have to drive for several days. Rest was a welcoming thought.

Hanging up, I gently moved Sportster, who had dozed off, from his snuggly spot on my chest. Of course this awoke and disturbed him and he wandered off in seek of another perfect spot of his choosing. I put the phone on charge and rummaged through the fridge for something to eat. Nothing sounded good when you were tired, and I was bone-tired. Of course the thought of turkey and dressing and all the fixin's, even though they would be leftovers, was enough to curb my appetite for a bowl of soup and a sandwich. Campbell's Chicken Noodle Soup and a ham sandwich was just what the doctor ordered to satisfy my hunger and soothe my soul. A hot shower, jammies, and a good book finished the prescription for a good night's sleep. Before I knew it, my eyelids became heavy and I drifted into slumber with the sound of purrs from the warm fur ball curled by my ear, and I dreamt of pumpkin pies and turkey.

Chapter Eight

Traveling south on I-95 and moving along with traffic, I was feeling good, as I knew this was my last day on the road. I would see my friend, Vickie, and her family today, and get a rest from driving. And then suddenly in front of me a spectacular scene takes my breath away. The Atlantic Ocean! I knew I would see it but I was just not prepared for its impact, its significance.

It was sparkling blue-green with small white caps that represented a cool breeze across the water. I saw a couple of sail boats, their white sails pointing to the Florida sun. I was overwhelmed by what this scene signified. I had driven from the Pacific Ocean to the Atlantic Ocean! I had driven across this entire great country of ours, from sea to shining sea. God bless America! My heart swelled and tears filled my eyes as the emotion overcame me. This was the land that I loved, from the mountains, to the valleys, to the oceans, white with foam.... I realized I was singing at the top of my lungs as the tears flooded down my cheeks. Sportster lifted his head from sleep and stared at me in concern. I ordered him to take note of this moment in his life and reminded him that not many kitties had traveled from one coast to the other, and that he was one lucky cat. Jack Incarnate was quiet but I could tell he was fighting back his own emotions as he gazed out the window.

I couldn't stop crying as I became aware of the significance of this instant. Everything had come together in this one moment in time. The struggles and stress of a difficult relationship, the loss of my beloved, were all in this one moment. This moment belonged to the past and yet it was the future. Right now I-95 was the gateway to everything in the future. From here I could go anywhere, do everything. I was full of gratitude for all who have graced my life and molded me. But most of all I sent a silent prayer of thanks to Jack. *Your life is done but far from over because you live through me now. As sure as our lives have mixed and blended, I am the best of you and the best of me. I could not have done this without you. God bless you.*

I continued south on I-95, so close to my destination I could taste it. The congested traffic caused the hours to pass slowly, but periodically my emotions spiked at the glimpses of the Atlantic Ocean. At four in the afternoon, I was glancing at my handwritten directions: right turn, go two blocks, turn left, third house on the left. I had arrived! My heart was beating like a thousand drumrolls. No sooner did I pull up to the curb and shut off the engine, than Vickie burst out the front door, followed by her husband Max, whose big hand held a tiny mittened and that belonged toMakayla, their daughter. What a sight! Her daughter was the tiniest version of Vickie and Max. And Max! If he wasn't already attached…. He could have played the double for Kenny Rogers.

In that moment, the history of our relationship started rolling like a newsreel. Vickie was just twenty-one when I met her. Her face was framed by long brown hair with bangs that hid a worried wrinkle. A small nose and big blue eyes reminded me of a doll. She laughed hesitantly, as if unsure of the humor. She always lived on the serious side of life. When she came to me for a job, she had moved back with her mom and stepfather as she recovered from a divorce. But even then she was an independent soul. At twenty-one, divorced, and starting over (if one can say starting over at such a young age), she was broke but full of visions for the future.

The first day to work she pulled up in front of the shop in a dented-up old Volkswagen her older brother had nursed back to health. At the end of that day of nerves and new beginnings, she lifted the hood of her treasured piece of transportation, and with dirty rag in hand, checked the oil before she headed home. It wasn't long before she moved on up the scale to reliable transportation and brought a brand-new bright red Chevy pickup truck. She had needed the truck to pull the horse trailer she had also purchased, because she had acquired a horse and had begun riding with a volunteer posse group, associated with the sheriff's department, who did strenuous riding on weekends in training for rescues and disasters.

She never ceased to amaze me with her spirit and ambition. When she decided to get involved in a new interest she bought books and studied, examining every angle of the new endeavor before she set foot on the new adventure. And as brave and as adventurous as she was, she was soft-spoken and shy. When I first met her, I used to think if I yelled "Boo!" she'd turn tail and run, but I learned quickly that her timid demeanor hid a strong, brave, stubborn streak that surged just below the surface. I envied her youth and focus, wishing I had been as collected and driven when I was her age.

Vickie had left California, what was it, six years ago to move to Florida to remarry her ex-husband? She had just divorced the ex for the first time when she had come to me, applying for a job. She had been twenty-one. Now she was forty-one. The remarriage didn't work out, but she finally found her soul mate and married Max, who agreed to have the baby that Vickie had desired all her life. Max was ten years older, divorced, mature, and quiet. As he came out of the house and crossed the lawn, with his big hand gently encircled around his little girl's finger, you knew instantly he was there for the long haul.

Their marriage was put to the supreme test when Makayla had been born four month's premature, weighing only fifteen ounces. That was less than a pound of hamburger. She was a miracle child, nurtured by her loyal parents as she laid in her incubator for four months, fighting for life every breath along the way. Weeks passed before they were allowed to even caress their newborn, because a preemie's brain could overload just from the stimulus of touch. The local news covered little Makayla's progress as she battled every inch of her tiny life until, finally, after four months of hospitalization, parental agony, and millions of prayers, she was able to go home.

My friend Vickie was the only one I knew who could have dealt with the strain of those months. I had always admired that she was made of "the right stuff." I remember the day she walked into my business looking for a job. She didn't know how to groom, but, she added, she was eager to learn. She timidly explained she had done crafts that required scissoring frayed yarn into little round balls. She was a natural, acquiring the grooming skills quickly and easily. Within months I was allowing her to groom alone on Mondays, giving me a day off. I knew she was scared to death with the responsibility and, although Jack would be there acting as a receptionist, she later admitted she was intimidated by him too. But she did it and asked every question conceivable of the grooming business. She hustled because I hustled. There were many times as the business grew that we worked six and seven days a week. She learned the secret of a successful business: never turn down an appointment. And we became friends. She struggled through the shreds of her marriage and strove for independence from her loving but needy mother, and I dealt with the difficulties of my relationship with Jack. Her mother had divorced her alcoholic father when Vickie was a baby. After getting to know Jack's story of recovery, she was able to muster up the courage to call her dad and meet with him. She still maintains a relationship to this day, not a close one, but she knows her dad.

After almost thirteen years under my employ, she made the move to Florida to reunite with her ex-husband. I cried for days after she left and wondered how I would survive without her: the ideal employee, but most of all, my best friend. In a short time, she started her own mobile dog-grooming business. The phone line to and from Florida was busy while I mentored her as she handled difficult customers and situations. Her business flourished even though her remarriage failed for the second time.

And here we were, twenty years later from that first day. I stood in her front yard, hugging and exchanging tears of relief and joy. All the firsts and the lasts, the past and the future and everything in between, were in this moment. We released each other and I turned, reaching out my hand to Max. "Judy, I have heard so much about you."

As he reached out his hand, his other still snug around Makayla's little hand, he smiled an easy smile. "I am sure you have." He knew that Vickie and I talked long distance all the time, dissecting every difficulty in our lives, the difficulties being Jack and Max.

"Well, come on in, Thanksgiving dinner is ready and waiting." Vickie herded her beloved flock back to the house. On the table was everything you could imagine. The ham sat crusty-sweet with brown sugar and cloves. And turkey too! It perched in the table's middle, crispy, golden with white slices still dripping with juices. The mound of mashed potatoes with green flecks of parsley was positioned next to the yellow yams with a toasted marshmallow topping. What a spread!

We feasted with food and conversation. The chatter at the table moved easily from one subject to another and if it stalled, there was always the input of a three-year-old to keep everyone laughing and smiling. The banquet sped by, disappearing into tummies already full to overflowing, leaving only bones and dishes scraped clean. I helped Vickie with the cleanup and marveled that this was the twenty-one-year-old girl who had entered my life so long ago, now with a business, a home, a husband, and the cutest little girl. We retired to the living room, sharing pictures and stories, until the food and warmth sedated me with yawns and heavy eyelids. It had been such a long, eventful day. A day I will never forget. A Thanksgiving I will never forget.

We all said our goodnights with hugs and sleep-tights, and I headed out to the curb where my warm bed welcomed me. Jack Incarnate was sound asleep and did not hear me come in, but Sportster met me at the door, purring and happy to see me. I felt a contentedness I had not felt since I had started this trip. The rough roads, the tornados, the perilous bridges, all had left me with rough edges that the affection and caring of my friend smoothed out with her tenderness.

After locking the door, I scooped up Sportster and hugged him tightly, smelling his scent and feeling his warm fur against my face. I could have hugged him for a lifetime, but he tolerated only a minute before he squirmed out of my arms, chattering about his conversation with Jack Incarnate while I was having dinner. Evidently Jack Incarnate was upset with the twenty-five-hundred miles of road dirt on the motor home and, he had pointed out, the oil would need changing.

I climbed into my pj's and snuggled into the bedcovers; Sportster's purrs filled my ear as I scratched a list of things to do. Max had already made an appointment for the oil change in the morning, so I would catch up on my laundry and visit with Vickie while he took the Wizard to the garage. When he returned I would wash it and do my own housecleaning: the floors, windows, making the bed, and changing the litter. All would be shipshape by evening, when they took me to The Dolly Parton's Dixie Stampede, a dinner-theater extravaganza.

I slept with the contentedness of a job well done. I didn't contemplate the looming chore of a twenty-five-hundred mile return trip; that would be for another day. Tonight, tucking me in and feathering my forehead like a loving kiss, was the warm full feeling of good food, the calming closeness of a friend and her family, and the glow of an achievement. Those mixtures of sweet sensations enveloped me like a down comforter and I slept a dreamless sleep.

Florida's early morning sun trumpeted its golden rays around the motor home's window shades and sang a glorious melody to the inhabitants snuggled inside. Without opening my eyes, I stretched to the revelry and, feeling the warm lump by my side, tried not to disturb Sportster. Jack Incarnate was already awake and ready for the day's promise. I could sense his eagerness as it matched the momentum of the morning sun's ballet in the eastern horizon.

I slowly pulled back the covers, found Sportster's furry little face squinting with sleep, and laid a big fat kiss on top of his head. "We're burning daylight!" He only looked at me with indignation, probably thinking, *"I'll get up when I am ready. How dare you attempt to arrange my schedule!"* I laughed out loud at his reply and punched the coffee button. I didn't know what time Vickie's household started stirring but I doubted it was at daybreak. I dressed and made the bed, leaving the lump in the middle, and checked the news from my L.A. feed on my satellite dish. It was cold and raining back home, with traffic accidents and backups as the mall parking lots filled with early holiday shoppers trying to catch the best Black Friday deals.

I was wired up, not from the caffeine, but maybe just from six days of jumping up, driving, and sightseeing. The thought of kicking back and being shown around town was appealing.

Suddenly I remembered Max had the appointment for my motor home's oil change. I began
stowing things away and then began to strip the
bed. Sportster was not pleased but said he was
getting up anyway. He jumped to the floor, padded to the front, and without asking, used Jack
Incarnate's lap as a springboard to the dash and
then quietly surveyed the morning's offerings. I
stuffed the last of my dirty clothes into the second
pillowcase and set them by the door. I pulled up
the shades and decided Sportster had the right
idea. I grabbed my coffee cup, plopped onto the
couch, and gazed out the window.

The neighborhood was just waking up. I counted
five vehicles parked at the house across the street.
Two had out-of-state license plates: family, home
for the holidays. I watched as a woman, still in her
flannel nightgown, chilled by the dawn's brisk air,
hurried out the front door to the Ford truck with the
Virginia plates in the driveway. Unlocking the cab
door, she grabbed a bag, and I heard the thunk
of the truck door slamming as she quickly trotted
back into the warmth of the house. Two houses
down a man bundled in work clothes climbed into
his car and, though I couldn't hear the engine fire
up, I saw the white smoke spew from the exhaust
pipe as it hit the chilly atmosphere. Then, minutes later I heard the hum of the car's engine as
it crept past my window, the sound melding with
first light's hush.

The comings and goings of ordinary people,
sharing with family and friends, going to work,
and making a home. The routine was the same

from coast to coast, everyone making a life, raising their children, and being thankful and free to come and go. I wondered in how many countries this scene from my window could not play out. I was filled with gratitude and joy to live in the USA. A tap on my door brought me out of my reverie.

"Judy? Are you up?"

"Oh. sure. Come on in!" I jumped up, took one step, and opened the door. Vickie stepped inside with her own cup of coffee.

"Everyone's still asleep. How did you sleep?"

"Like a rock. It just feels so good to be here. And the dinner was fantastic, by the way. And little Makayla is such a doll! Does she ever stop talking? I got such a kick out of Max dealing with her. I asked him yesterday if he ever gets a word in. He said, 'Most of the time, no.'"

"Yes, he's really great with her. I'm really lucky."

"And he is not a stranger to the kitchen, either. I am impressed."

"He does a lot of the cooking. In fact, I think he's a better cook than I am. He did most of the dinner yesterday. And he's usually home from work before I am, so he starts dinner and I clean up after."

"Well, I am impressed."

"So you want to come in the house? Max will be up soon and will make breakfast."

"Sure. I have my laundry all together."

"Good. I'll help you carry it in."

Breakfast was eggs and bacon and more than any of us needed after the Thanksgiving feast.

Makayla woke up chattering. I wondered if she had stopped when her eyes closed last night.

"I unplugged the satellite dish and the electrical cord and I'll bring Sportster in the house in his carrier til you get back from the oil change."

"Great. I'll be going in a minute. The appointment's at nine."

"When you get back, I'd like to wash it. I can't believe the road dirt on it. You don't have to help. I like doing it myself and the exercise will feel good on this nice day."

"Oh, okay," he answered, a little unsure that his gentlemanly manners would not be called upon.

After Max was on his way, Vickie got me started with my laundry and hers too and we chatted nonstop about everything and anything as we sorted and folded. The sun was high and warm in the sky when Max returned, and I took on the task of washing the motor home. Vickie and Makayla made a trip to the store and returned to make turkey sandwiches for lunch. There was nothing like Thanksgiving leftovers and it was hard not to stuff myself again. After a nap in the afternoon, we had just enough time to dress for dinner. We were going out to a dinner theater at Dolly Parton's Dixieland Stampede. I donned my jeans, boots, and cowboy hat for the occasion, and little Makayla was adorable in pink cowboy boots and hat. When Max's fifteen-year-old son, Luke, arrived, it was nice to finally meet him, as I had heard so much about him through Vickie.

The dinner and show was great! Seated in a circular forum like an arena, we looked down on a rodeo-style setting that entertained us with horses and their riders performing fantastic gymnastics and formations. The drinks were served in a free souvenir glass mug shaped like a cowboy boot.

The story of the Dixie Stampede Carriage Room goes like this: "Years ago there was an old carriage house in the foothills of the Great Smokey Mountains that became a gathering spot for local folks to get together for food, drinks, and fun. Every night when the sun went down, northern and southern folks alike would hitch their horses outside, bring in their stools to sit on, and eagerly await some cool refreshment and the night's entertainment.

"The Carriage Room was so unique that you would find Confederate and Union troops clappin' and stompin' and laughin' together. The news of all the fun became widespread and soon people from all parts would ride into town just to hear the banjo pickin' and the fiddlin' competitions. They were even known to hold contests of skill like wrestlin', ropin', and even dancin'.

"Of course, things could have easily gotten out of hand with the combination of Confederate and Union troops in that one little spot. So to prevent any trouble, a special menu of drinks was created. Legend has it that the Carriage Room became so popular, that when the last mug was gone, patrons would start drinking out of their own boots."

As much as I enjoyed the show, I more enjoyed watching little Makayla with her pink cowboy hat, as she giggled with glee at Santa on horseback and the clowns falling off horses. It was a wonderful night. Lucas seemed to have his head on straight and possessed the same quiet calmness of his father. It was late when we pulled into the drive. With hushed goodnights and hugs, Max carried his sleeping daughter into the house, while Vickie and Lucas carted souvenir boot mugs, pink cowboy hat, and leftovers inside. I headed once again for my welcoming Sportster and warm bed.

Slipping into bed I thought of the memorable day and the comfort of friends. Another good day completed with the promise of sleeping in tomorrow.

I awoke at seven Florida time and showered and dressed. Today was sightseeing day and I was excited to see, of all things, a motel that Jack had told Max he had once stayed. It was our first stop: Anthony's on the Beach Motel in Cocoa Beach. I jumped out and took a quick picture, and later wished I had walked down to the beach just like Jack had done so many years ago. I just wanted to connect with some now faint, shadowy ghost of Jack's presence. A tear leaked down my cheek as we drove away, and Makala in her car seat next to me watched it slide down my chin. "What's wrong Grandma Judy? Are you sad?" The innocence of the three-year-old touched me as I answered, "No, honey, I was just remembering my Jack."

"Grandpa Jack?"

"Yes, honey."

"Oh." That one word encompassed the quiet subdued understanding of a three-year-old.

Next we drove by Cape Canaveral Space Center, and then stopped at Rocky Point Campground and walked on the pier. I picked up a perfect rock off the beach for my souvenir rock collection. They then took me to the house they were building. We clomped through the skeleton of wood frames as they described each room's potential features. It was going to be a beautiful large home. We stopped for lunch at a beachfront restaurant and then headed home. It was time for naps for Makayla and us big people. Later Vickie and I snuck out to Wal-Mart while Makayla and Max still slept. I bought a Miami Dolphins sweatshirt, for my manager's husband, at a much better price than at a tourist shop.

We had dinner that evening with Vickie's brother Rickie and his family.

Startled, I realized that time had turned "Little Rickie," the name I had always called him, into a responsible, polite young man. The learning disabilities he had as a child had not interfered with his success in raising and supporting his family. The noisy seafood restaurant on the beach entertained us with good music and dancing. I had fun watching youngsters (I can now call them that, now that I am an old widow) dance and drink, not yet touched by losses and hardships. The evening wound down and, after saying my well-wishes to Ricky and his family, we headed home.

Sunday morning promised to be a brisk, clear, puffy-cloud day. They were taking me on an air-boat ride. The experience made me think back to those rivers and swamps I had crossed. I was going to get up close and personal. We climbed onto the airboat and our captain began hand-ing out what I thought were earphones, but which ended up only being ear protection from the loud roar of the airboat's motor. We cruised the river without seeing any alligators, but we did witness lots of other wildlife. It was scenic and unforget-table. We returned home, dropped Max off, and Vickie, Makayla, and I headed for an annual art show in Cocoa. I found a rusty lawn sculpture that reminded me of the Quartzite Campground. The sculpture was a Snoopy dog wearing a cowboy hat and cradling a shotgun in his arms. I proba-bly paid too much, but after walking away twice, I came back, bit the bullet, and we carted him back to the car. I couldn't wait to get him home on my patio.

Again the day wound down and we had a quiet dinner at home. I listened with the patience of a grandparent to Makayla's stories of owies and wishes for Santa. Max shared some of his Alan Jackson CDs with me, and I was filled with awe as we watched a video after dinner of a local news-reel of Makayla's hospital stay and her valiant fight for life. I shared a tape I had of Jack as a speaker at an AA meeting, during a time when we had been separated. Cleaning out drawers and cup-boards, I had found the tape a month after his death. He spoke of his life, his drinking, his sobriety and our relationship, and his hope that we would reunite.

That night as I lay awake, unable to sleep, I thought of all the happenings of the last several days, knowing that tomorrow was my last day before I headed back to California. Yes, I had made it all the way across the country, but what about everyday life when I returned? How would I go on? Would I keep my nose to the grindstone without Jack cheering me on? Would I know how to budget the bills and bolster my bank account? How would I do it all alone? Who would watch my back? For so many years I knew no one would mess with me with my tough Harley guy by my side. I was safe. And now I was on my own.

But I was not alone. Jack was in my heart and in my soul. I heard his voice at every turn. All that lecturing and domineering guidance was ingrained in me. I would not forget. But I was still so afraid as I got ready to head back home to reality. Having tossed and turned until dawn, I finally wore out the subject and dozed off to a fitful slumber.

Morning came as I heard Max leaving for work first, and then Vickie taking Makayla to day care. There was time to get dressed and savor a cup of coffee before Vickie returned. We would have this last day to ourselves for girl talk.

The day passed too quickly. I rode with Vickie as she did errands and then took me on a tour through the town of St.Augustine, an ancient town known for the discovery of the Fountain of Youth by the explorer Ponce De Leon. The town's architecture and ambiance lured us into a time of Spanish occupancy and culture as we cruised through its streets. Lack of time prevented us from stopping at many of the historical sites, as we had to pick up Makayla from day care and head home. We had a simple dinner that evening, with subdued conversation. Even Makayla was quieter than normal, as my last hours with them faded into tearful tight hugs and goodnights. Vickie and Max would head out for work in the morning, and I would begin the end of my adventure. The first mile of the last of my trip.

Oddly, I realized I couldn't wait to get home. I was homesick. I wanted the familiarity of my home, my town, my friends, and my business. I wanted to drive the streets I knew and watch my neighbors come and go in their daily routines. I wanted to drive by the golf course in the early morning and see the groups of golfers huddled around the tee in the brisk fall atmosphere, exhaling vapor puffs and hugging themselves for warmth. And I wanted to feel the warm California sun melt the chill from the air as I hiked the hills that were turning green from the winter's rains.

I wanted to have lunch at the restaurant where I knew the waitress' names and have an ice cream cone at the drug store where everyone gathered on hot summer nights. I missed the variety of golf carts and motorized chairs that putted along their own private lane, carrying the seniors to their destinations of doctors, banks, grocery stores, and golf courses. I wanted to go home.

Jack Incarnate murmured, *"You can't just click your heels together now. You have a long* way to go before you get home. I told you before, Judy, no matter how far you go, home is always "home". And he was so surely right. Packing away things for the trek home, I watched Sportster watch me. He had learned the routine of travel and I knew he was aware that we were getting ready to roll again. He had become a real traveler and the question entered my mind, is he was going to want to travel again after such a long trip? Did he miss his home litter box? The view out the bedroom window? Going to work and taunting his doggie friends?

With all the souvenirs I had collected packed away, the storage under my couch was full of gifts. A T-shirt from Daytona's Harley Davidson for Jack's friend Blaine.

Blaine was there for Jack until the end. The sympathy card he'd sent had expressed his sentiments, "*It was always cars and Harleys with Jack and me. We could stand for hours in the garage, talking smack and polishing every inch of our bikes. I will never forget him.*"

Jack had arranged for him to purchase the bikes after his death. When the time came, I could not go into the garage without crying my eyes out and trying to avert my gaze from the bikes, parked like faithful companions, waiting for their beloved to return, slowly gathering a layer of dust.

Jack had secured a promise from Blaine to watch over me after he was gone, and Blaine, being the loyal devoted friend, had done just that. About once a week he called or stopped by the shop to ask how it was going. He had asked for some of Jack's ashes and placed them in a leather pouch attached to the gas tank of the Harley. "Now he can always ride," Blaine said as he choked back his emotions.

Blaine had been on my calling list on this trip. It was the least I could do for the man who had taken on this responsibility of watching over me. Surely he hadn't known I would be such a monumental task, driving cross-country and all.

I stowed two coffee cups from Big Bend National Park under the seat for my motor-home friends, John and Archie. They too were on my calling list and covered as my technical advisors for the trip. They had accumulated lots of experience traveling in their motor home every summer for years. So far they had to serve only as moral support and the true friends they were. They had been customers for years, and since Jack's death had helped to fill the vacuum of friendship that Jack had left. There had been no time for friends during Jack's all-consuming illness, and I was touched when they rallied up to the plate to fill the void of companionship.

My rusty Snoopy-dog sculpture was wrapped in towels and, since Jack Incarnate said, "*Absolutely not! That dog is not riding on my lap!*, I decided to secure the art form into the barrel chair by the door. My cowboy-boot mug was wrapped in the Miami Dolphins sweatshirt and stuffed under the bench seat with my other treasures, including my rock from Rocky Point.

Everything was secured and stowed away. My lists were checked to make sure nothing was forgotten. All was done that could be done that night. Crawling into bed almost reluctantly, I knew that tomorrow would be a full day on the road. The revisiting of those long, long bridges lay ahead, and who knew what else would be in store for me? A small shudder shook me and I pulled Sportster close, wishing he would tolerate a longer, crushing hug.

It seemed as if I had just closed my eyes when my last Floridian dawn lifted my lids open. The thought of the road ahead tightened a knot already in my stomach, and with dread I dragged myself out from under the covers. I quickly made the bed, dressed, and made an instant cup of coffee for the road. In the midst of rechecking my lists, Vickie approached, crossing the front lawn. I smiled and stepped outside. We hugged each other tightly.

"You drive careful. Alright?"

"Oh, I will. Thanks for a wonderful visit and a great Thanksgiving. And you guys have a wonderful Christmas too. Wish I could be here for that. Makayla's at that special magical age for Christmas."

"We will. And I'll miss you too. But remember we'll see each other again in September for the trade show in Las Vegas."

"Yes. And it'll be here before we know it."

"Well, I have to get to work."

"Yes, and I'm all ready to pull out. Guess this is it." We clutched each other one last time, both of us teary and sniffling. A tug on my jacket caused me to look down to see Makayla gazing up at me.

"G'bye, Grandma Judy." I bent down and gave her a big hug.

"Good-bye, Makayla. You take good care of your mommy and daddy, okay? And say hello to Santa for me."

"Okay." I laughed as they climbed into the car and drove away.

I took a deep breath, turned, and climbed into the driver's seat. Sportster was already perched on the dash in his co-navigator's position, while Jack Incarnate had his face turned away from me to hide his emotions.

Chapter Nine

Choked with emotion, I eased away from the curb as the Wizard choked too, spitting out exhaust, as I drove slowly to the end of the block, turned left, drove forward two more blocks, and turned right to reach the main road that would take me to I-95. The radio was tuned to a local station and the DJ talked of traffic and of stores that had opened at five a.m. with promises of savings galore for the early-bird Christmas shoppers.

"And today, folks, is the official end of hurricane season." Wow, was I glad to hear that! Approaching the on-ramp, I pressed the accelerator, urging the Wizardbb to pick up the pace, and listened to its engine's roar Was it protesting, dreading the long trip home? Perhaps Wizard too had enjoyed the time off. But reality and responsibilities waited at home. Cruising along the interstate, the odometer clicked off the miles like the pages of a calendar. Mile by mile and then day by day, and before I knew it, home would be a reality and this adventure would be a memory. My heart felt heavy considering the days ahead with just Jack Incarnate and Sportster. I would miss Vickie Max, and the chatter of little Makayla. Even with my sadness, the recollections warmed me.

It had been less than four months since Jack had gone from me and I first felt the sharp edge of emptiness. The moments when my life was full of togetherness filled my memory: our lying together in bed before succumbing to sleep, with my arm over his big shoulder, spooned next to his warmth. Then there were the nights I had laid on the bed's edge as far from him as possible, fuming over the day's argument that now, in the harsh light of emptiness, seemed such wasted moments. Wishing could not bring them back, and I knew somewhere in the great universe, Jack had come to a spiritual awakening that the harsh and critical words he had spewed on me were now an everlasting regret.

We ate our meals in front of the television, laughing at *Seinfield*, *Married with Children*, and *Everybody Loves Raymond*. How many times had I caught myself, alone and laughing out loud at a sitcom, and then suddenly aware there was no one to hear my laughter? Now, eating alone was just that, eating alone; it was not a "moment," But I could hear the echoes of the criticisms. *"You eat too fast. You don't even chew your food. You could survive in jail, alright. They only give you ten minutes to eat. You're going to have stomach problems some day. You need to chew your food."* In anger, I would then slowly chew each bite for five minutes, mocking him as he watched. And he would hold back his smile and say with a serious tone, *"There. That's how you should do it."*

There were so many "moments." He was so difficult. So many times, when I could take no more. It was those times, and it happened more than once, filled with anger and shattered feelings, that I would check into a local motel with nothing more than my purse and the clothes on my back. Although the room was stark, it was filled with solitude and safety from hurtful words, and I was never going home. But after several hours of solace and spiritual restoration, I didn't want him to worry about my whereabouts. I would call him and tell him I was never coming home again. I had had it. I would cry and vent and he would listen and hear. And after a night apart we would come back together, into each other's arms, both of us full of forgiveness. When we drove about town doing our errands, we would pass that local motel. He could never resist teasing, "There's Judy's room." With a glance at Jack Incarnate, I swore I heard a chuckle.

The Atlantic Ocean was shimmering on my right like a beacon, urging me on with reassurance that, this time, the way was not unknown. I had been this way before. Although the emptiness still stabbed my heart, I had endured four months and survived. So now the way was not new. And I would probably survive four more months, and then a year, and then two years…. Life would go on.

And life continued on, the engine humming, the tires beating a rhythm as they crossed the asphalt's cracks. Sportster was stretched out on his back, white soft tummy fur exposed to the warm sunshine streaming through the windshield. His little arms reaching out over his head, he slept soundly even as his head bobbled with the bumping movement as the motor home scrambled over rough spots in the road. Although the future held many more "firsts," and more "I've never done that before" and "I've never been there before," it did not concern Sportster. Life was good. And as I turned my head slightly, I am sure Jack Incarnate was considering the future. *"What will it be like when we return home? I know you. You are not going to sit still. And what about me? What is going to become of me?"*

His question spurred my thoughts. There were so many things I wanted to do. I had only dabbled in my oil painting over the years. I remembered when I first dipped my brush into the art. My second husband and I would go out in our dune buggy, driving through dry river beds, and climbing dunes to view the "nothing" as far as the eye could see. I acquired a new perspective of the delicate environment in that old converted Volkswagen bug that we had chopped and cropped. Many weekends the dune buggies required hours of maintenance in the garage. Those weekends the guys got greasy and the wives pouted in the kitchen with nothing to do.

It was then that I decided to take an oil painting class at the local adult education center. I became hooked, painting until all hours of the night, unable to stop the creative juices from flowing. I joined an art club and took informal lessons until the divorce forced me to funnel my finances and time into a mode of self-support. I had to get a job. The years had flowed by and I had experienced spurts of painting, but now I could concentrate on my passion. I could become immersed in it. I could redo the back bedroom to create an art studio. The picture formed in my mind as I drove along. Mentally I moved the old desktop that spanned two file cabinets from the garage. Jack had used it as a makeshift workbench. I moved it into the bedroom. It was not shiny-new, but presentable enough to be used as a craft desk and would not be worse for wear if the paints got on it. And the file cabinets could store my paint supplies. In my mind's picture, the walls would be like a gallery, displaying all my paintings. Mentally I built shelves in the closet for storing canvasses and more art supplies.

And what about that Art Expo in L.A. every year that I always yearned to attend? I could do that too. There was a Sun City Art Club I could join for inspiration and learning new techniques. Already I was planning trips to art festivals in my motor home and also visiting national parks and beautiful vistas to get inspiration for my new creations in oils and pastels.

My breathing quickened with excitement and my thoughts raced on. There were jobs around the house that needed to be done. The faded and frayed carpeting on the back patio needed replacing and the side patio, painted with green paint years ago, peeled from the hot summer sun and bared gray splotches of cement. I visualized brown ceramic tiles continuing from the side patio to the back, matching the house trim, and me, lounging on a porch swing with beautiful green potted plants adorning the area, their leaves swaying in the summer's evening breeze. My patio tables and chairs were pristine with a fresh coat of paint next to the barbeque grill. (Another skill to master.)The 1970's wallpaper throughout my house must be tackled in order to update the interior with fresh new paint in a color of the twenty-first century.

The miles clicked on as my mind was off and running. Jack's illness had stretched over two years, hindering me from the pleasure of sitting down to enjoy a good movie. Now I had the luxury of spending an hour, if I had to, at Blockbuster's, just to pick out a couple of movies.

I visualized a day of working in the yard, trimming and weeding, cleaning and sweeping the patio, washing the car, cleaning the garage. I saw myself dining at the patio table with a cold drink and a juicy cheeseburger I had cooked to perfection on the barbeque while watching the pinks and blues of a serene sunset, and later relaxing on the swing, surveying the day's accomplishments, and finally, retiring inside to watch a romantic "Judy" movie, as Jack had called them.

I wanted to learn line dancing. Since Jack had been gone, country music had filtered into my loneliness and softened the edges. Line dancing didn't require a partner and that suited me. I had a burning desire to see Kenny Chesney in concert.

It was not because he had won "Entertainer of the Year" for two years in a row, but because the first time I saw him perform on TV, I was mesmerized. His smooth baby face and baby-blue eyes captured me. As I watched his performance, there was an essence that mirrored Jack's, and I was sure if the two men's genealogy were researched we'd find they had shared some of the same ancestry. When I watched Kenny perform, my heart skipped a beat and I was in love. One of his hit songs, *Don't Blink,* told of an old man in his 102nd year, explaining that one day you are six years old and then you wake up and you have a high school sweetheart and finally you blink and you are celebrating your 50th wedding anniversary and praying God takes you first. *Life goes faster than you think*, he sang.

How could I be so excited about the future even though I would be alone? I pictured Jack Incarnate, alone and cold, staring through the windshield, sitting in the passenger seat of the Wizard parked alongside the house, gathering the dust of idleness. But my mind's images portrayed me taking control of my future and it gave me a sense of exhilaration and anticipation. I could take steps toward socializing. When I got home I could investigate RV clubs. Who knows, perhaps I could meet someone with similar interests…?

I pulled out of my reverie and realized the miles, not just the years, also go faster than I think. The first of the long bridges loomed in front of me,

The Jubilee Parkway. I quickly inhaled, hardly let up on the accelerator and approached the seven-mile span. I didn't exhale until I reached the western banks of Mobile Bay. Swelling with pride, I almost jumped up and down in my seat. Jack Incarnate gave me a look. *"Don't get too cocky, Judy You still have two more long bridges to go and I am not breathing til we are across them."*

I became frustrated, not for the first time. *"I don't have to listen to your negativity anymore. We have gone over twenty-five-hundred miles without a glitch. I don't need your 'under your breath' comments, Jack Incarnate! I can unplug you, too! If something happens, we'll deal with it. Otherwise, shut up!"*

"Well, you don't want me to remind you of the past, do you? Sometimes you just don't think" I knew what he was talking about without his elaborating. The "unplugging incident" that eventually led to my "overconfident incident" flashed to the forefront of my mind.

Jack had bought a Honda Goldwing touring bike during our early days together. He thought he could shed his past and his Harley roots. I guess he believed that the Honda would wipe clean the pages of his past. We joined the Goldwing Association and Jack made a valiant attempt to socialize with its members. It didn't take long before Jack became thoroughly frustrated as he tried to ride with them. They were "too nice," wore clean-cut Dockers, and had too many rules for group riding, including a list of hand signals.

They rode too fast on mountain roads, and at restaurant stops there were always the impatient riders who wanted to resume riding before the rest of the group was finished eating. It didn't take long before Jack tired of trying to fit in.

So we rode alone, when the weather was perfect and not a cloud in the sky. Riding a bike in the rain was not only dangerous, but also there was a lot of chrome to clean up after the ride, and Jack didn't like messes. But there were gorgeous weekends, and we took advantage of those days. I loved sitting behind Jack on my cushioned seat with armrests as my helmet, with earphones built in, piped either music or Jack's voice to my ears. The smell of pine on a mountain ride, or the aroma of fresh-cut hay from a passing semi hauling bales to a local ranch, stirred my senses and made me feel alive.

The fact that we could converse with each other through the microphones in our helmets didn't mean that the conversations were always "Oohs" and "aahs" and "Oh, look at that!" I remember one time in particular when we had been on a ride with the Goldwing group. Jack had become totally frustrated with the riders, their hand signals, and their speed going up a mountain road. The frustration was funneled through that microphone to my ears, and no amount of my "I understands" or "I know how you feels" could make it better. He finally pulled away from the group and we headed home on our own. We hit the flatlands and ended up on the interstate near the marine base at Camp Pendleton.

I sat quietly, Jack still blaring his complaints into my helmet about the situation, when I watched him make an unsure exit.

"Is this the right exit?" he asked.

"Uhm. I'm not sure." I really wasn't sure until seconds later when I saw the sign "Camp Pendleton Marine Base Entrance." *"Oh oh. This is not good."* I was not going to say anything. It really was too late anyway. My input would have only fueled his rantings that were going to crescendo soon enough. Obviously he didn't see the sign because he said nothing, even when he saw the guardhouse with a smartly uniformed, white-gloved *armed* Marine.

"What is your business on the base, sir?"

"I guess I made a wrong turn back there." I could feel Jack's embarrassment turning into hot anger.

"Okay, sir. You can make a U-turn there and that will take you back to the interstate. Have a good day, sir." Jack quietly made the U-turn and headed the bike back in the direction we had come before he unleashed his mortification.

"Why didn't you say something?!" He yelled. "You know I can't ride and read all the signs too! What good are you, sitting back there? Why don't you…?"

I reached down to the side of the bike and unplugged my earphones. Almost sweet silence. I could still hear his muffled voice over the engine's rumble and the road noise, but the sharp, cutting, hurtful words swept on past me with the wind. Miles farther down the road, he pulled into a roadside food stand for a cold drink and, I was sure, to unwind a bit. I confessed to him that I had unplugged him and he sputtered in disbelief, suddenly aware that his rantings had been wasted on the wind, unheard. And then he laughed.

He told that story many times over the years that when I don't want to listen, I just unplug him.

The unplugging incident led me to the overconfident incident. Even if I discounted his complaining attitude, I also tired of his precise rules in which we only rode when the weather was perfect or he was in the right mood. Thus the crazy idea was born: I wanted my own bike to ride when I wanted. Perhaps we could go more often on our own, since we could ride with each other. Someone in the club had a bike with a sidecar and even a little tent trailer to tow behind the bike, all match-painted and priced right.

I had to have a sidecar because my short legs would not reach the ground as I straddled the bike. Tour bikes were too heavy to lean to the side and hold up with one leg. If guys dropped their bikes they required help getting them back up off the ground.

Cash was exchanged and Jack rode the bike home. He pulled into the garage and examined our purchase more closely. We opened up the tent and proceeded to clean and polish every inch of our new toy. Jack began explaining gears and hand brakes, and clutches and throttles. I listened carefully as he cautioned me to go slowly and practice shifting the gears. He warned that even a bike with a sidecar could tip over easily if the rider took a curve too fast.

I mounted the bike and turned the key. It rumbled to life. I eased out of the driveway and onto the country road in front of our house in low gear. Jack trotted alongside as I tried second gear. Then third. I was doing it! I pulled away from Jack. I was now putt-putting at an easy pace, downshifting, then upshifting, up and down the road. The thrill of accomplishment made my heart race. Twenty minutes passed as Jack observed anxiously from our front porch while I purred along the maze of roads in the valley below our house. I made a pass by our house, smiling and waving with the confidence of a leather-worn, iron-butt biker who had ridden since birth. I headed for a sharp turn a quarter of a mile down the road from that confident gesture.

Ahead was a right curve, and a ten-feet-high wall of granite towered on the roadside's left edge, leaving no shoulder. The turn was sharp, as the road squeezed past the looming rock embankment. The sky was blue with white puffy clouds. It was a perfect eighty degrees. A slight breeze carried the aroma of sagebrush from the hills.

As I headed into the turn I was sure I felt the sidecar tipping and Jack's words of warning flashed into my mind. Perhaps I was taking the turn a little too fast. The hand brake was on the same handlebar as the throttle. Inexperience caused me to twist the throttle as I tried to squeeze the brake. The bike surged forward. I gasped at the rock barrier that was quickly approaching. I was now going even faster, with no control over the pretty bike with its sidecar and its perfectly match-painted tent trailer at home in the garage.

Directly in front of me was a sheer impending mountain of granite. The road had disappeared around the curve and gone on without me. There was only one thing to do: abandon ship. Just inches before those last pretty seconds of the bike's life, I threw my body to the side, hitting the asphalt and loose gravel, skidding, as my jeans and new biker boots shredded their fabric and leather across the road's pavement. As my body came to a stop, I watched as my shiny new toy of steel and fiberglass, cleaned and polished, chrome sparkling in the sun, continued on without me as it ascended that rock embankment as if it truly did have "goldwings." It reached the top of the wall, lost its momentum, hung for what seemed like an eternity in the mid-eighty-degree sage-scented air, then did a slow motion somersault against the backdrop of blue sky and puffy clouds, and floated featherlike back to earth.

The loud report of the impact ended the pretty bike's life and echoed throughout the valley and up to Jack's ears. He stood on the front porch, unable to see around the corner for the cause of the sonic boom. He began running as he feared I had been hit by a car. I leapt up from my position on the pavement, unaware of any injuries, raced to the bend in the road to appear in full sight of Jack, and began waving my arms above my head. "I'm okay!" I yelled. Even at that distance I could see the relief in his face as he slowed to a quick walk, out of breath from panic. He came around the bend and surveyed the bike's dead body as it lay at the base of the granite wall, its broken bits of fiberglass and windshield strewn across the road.

Upon hearing the crash our neighbor down the road came running up behind Jack. Rick had five acres and two young boys who rode dirt bikes. As Rick surveyed the damage, Jack announced, "$500.00 and it's all yours. It comes with a match-painted tent trailer."

"Great! I'll take it!" He pushed the bike down to his house and my bike days were officially over. It was never spoken of again. Well, except every time we drove past that fateful corner. Jack would point out the broken pieces of windshield and fiberglass that lay by the roadside.

"There's Judy's bike." I could still hear the relief in his laugh. And Jack Incarnate snickered.

Chapter Ten

Jack Incarnate shook his head at my bike-riding memories with a smile that twisted the fabric of his cotton face. *"You never listened to me."*

"I listened a lot of times," I heard myself shout out loud. Sportster rolled his head from his upside-down position, his eyes opened to slits. I felt the flush of embarrassment. I was getting carried away in an argument with no one.

It was over ten years later. The broken pieces of my bike-riding days had been washed away by the rains and ground into the roadside dirt. The Honda days were over. Jack, however, had wanted "one more Harley before I die." It was a Softail Custom with a flame paint job, double spokes on the wheels, and a narrow cold chrome rail of a seat for the passenger. There were no cushy armrests or earphones piping pop rock into the helmet. I never desired to perch my plump butt cheeks on the thin rack this bike offered. That picture would not appease the eye, like some bikers do with their twenty-year-old, tanned blonde passengers, who sported black leather bikini tops and tight leather chaps hugging firm young bottoms just above their indecency. The bike's expensive paint job made Jack nervous anytime I came near it. He didn't want my booted foot swinging over it or anywhere near it. So the feelings were mutual: I didn't want on it and he didn't want me near it.

Many Saturdays, when free hot dogs and Cokes were the menu at the Harley dealership, Jack would want to hang out. He would drag me out of the car to join him as he would ogle the new Harleys, examine each and every bike in the parking lot, and talk chrome and fishtail pipes, and I would patiently stand by my man and try to act interested. With the trend shifting to more and more women riding their own bikes, the conversation turned to my one failed attempt.

"You should take a riding class, Judy that's what I did." She had long straight raven-black hair that matched the black leathers she was poured into. "Really! It's six weeks long and they teach you everything," she encouraged.

"Yeah." Her friend chimed in. "That's what we all did. Then you know just what to do." I began to get excited. Maybe I could ride after all.

It wasn't so much that I really wanted to ride, but it was that Jack and I would have something to do together. I could see Jack's eyes darting nervously as he considered an exit at the thought of me trying to ride again. He didn't make any comments about the new suggestion that day. The following weekend we took a drive out to visit the location of the classes. We watched from the sidelines as an employee explained in detail. We decided I would sign up. Well, I decided. Jack silently went along with my choice. There was a three-month waiting list for weekend classes, so he probably felt he didn't have to panic, yet.

A few weeks later, we were hanging out at the Harley dealership, browsing the showroom floor. Jack pointed out a Harley Sportster, a small bike, perfect for me. Now I knew Jack was not in favor of my riding, but he also could not resist a good excuse to have a second Harley in his garage. He would have bought a hundred Harleys if he had the money and the room and then a hundred more show cars too. It was always bikes and cars with Jack. So by the end of the day the new little Sportster was tucked away in the garage, waiting for its owner to complete riding classes.

As the days passed and the classes neared, Jack became more and more agitated with the idea of my riding again. Whenever I did something careless or stupid he didn't hesitate to inform me: "You have to be always on the alert when you are riding. You can't let your mind wander. I know you, Judy, you don't always pay attention." These tirades would occur at least on a weekly basis, until finally, one day, I caved. The truth be told, I really didn't want to be a biker. I had just wanted to do something with Jack and secretly I agreed with Jack. I didn't think I had the acumen for riding a motorcycle.

"Okay. I'll withdraw from the waiting list and get my deposit back." Two months of worry drained from his face. I hadn't realized how tense he had been. I made up flyers for my Harley and posted them at work and around town. As the weeks passed no takers stepped up to relieve me of my abandoned whim.

How we ended up at the RV sales lot I can't recall, but as playful Lookey Lou's, we browsed the interiors of campers, fifth wheels, and huge diesel pushers. As the salesman pointed out features and the advantage that an RV was a write-off as a second home, the lighthearted banter turned serious. We began to consider the different amenities and prices, narrowing our now-serious search down to a Class C type. Not too long, but long enough for a permanent bed on the ground floor so we wouldn't have to climb a ladder to a bed over the cab. The twenty-four-foot Winnebago Itasca was perfect. It was like new and had a V-10 engine. As we started to become emotional, we had to take a step back. I was still making payments on my Harley. We joked with the salesman, "How about taking a Harley for a down payment?"

"I'll check with my boss." What? They were going to consider it? We were just joking. I'd bet the owner was just another macho male, his favorite movie being *Easy Rider,* and a sucker for a Harley, because, by day's end, my Harley Sportster had a new home and we were proud owners of a

Winnebago Itasca Spirit. It was twenty-four feet of fiberglass with sweeping blue and purple designs on its sides, fully self-contained with subtle browns and mauves decorating the interior, just perfect for two. From that day on, Jack would point to his Harley and say, "That's my baby." He would then point to the motor home and say, "That's her baby." He was so right.

As I drove along, and the long, long, bridge neared, I recalled the maiden voyage in our new motor home to Santa Cruz and the redwoods. We were both green when it came to motor home travel. Jack had a motor home many years ago, when everything was manual. If you wanted hot water you had to go outside to light the pilot on the water heater. There was no forced-air furnace, no microwave or flushing toilet. But now we were traveling in style. With a push of the button, the water heater would click on and with a turn of the thermostat we had forced-air heat. After traveling the first several hours, I remember the thrill of using my own bathroom, avoiding the usually unsanitary facilities at the rest stops.

Our first stop was Montana de Oro State Park. A winding tree-lined road led us off the interstate to a campground with spacious campsites but no hookups. A short walk led to a sandy beach with tide pools. That night was the darkest and quietest night I had ever experienced. We awoke to a glorious daybreak and, peeking out the bedroom window, we witnessed a cougar prowling the area. How exciting! After a cup of instant coffee we headed back to the interstate.

We had heard what a beautiful drive the 101 can be, and decided to stay off the interstate and experience the famous scenery. We traveled along the shoreline for miles, enjoying scenery we had seen only in movies, on postcards, and in commercials. It was absolutely breathtaking. But suddenly, before we realized, the road that had been only two lanes was now hanging on the side of a cliff that dropped to the ocean floor three hundred feet below. I gasped and clung to my armrest on my passenger-side door that was inches from the rock wall. If Jack made one wrong twist of the steering wheel to the right, we would scrape the cliff's wall, or worse, to the left, we would be over the edge and plummeting to our deaths in the churning surf below. We now realized that the road climbed and twisted around the mountain like a snake climbing up a tree. We both cried out when we saw a big tour bus a quarter of a mile ahead, coming around the bend. How could there be room for us to pass each other? But Jack, with his iron grip on the wheel, held it steady as the giant bus whooshed past. We laughed and exhaled together as we realized we had made the tight squeeze.

There was silence in the motor home. No more oohs and aahs. Just concentration. There were short comments when the view was so spectacular it demanded comment, but mostly our eyes were glued to the road with only quick darting glances to the deadly drop below. As we rounded another curve, we came upon a bridge with orange cones and workers, their work trucks squeezed along the roadside. Jack slowed as we approached the bridge and just as we began to cross the span, then *rat-a-tat, rat-a-tat*! The sound of a jackhammer sent jolts of pure terror through our bones. I think we both yelled at the same time before we realized the bridge was not collapsing under us into the sea below. Again we exhaled and laughed at our fear, like kids taunting each other during a midnight walk in a shadowy alley. Finally we came to a restaurant and eagerly pulled off the road into the parking lot. Relieved to stop and unwind, we entered the log-cabin-style restaurant. Inside was a massive stone fireplace with cozy rustic redwood furniture inviting the visitor to sit a spell on a cold winter night. We were shown a table in the back and ordered coffee. The entire back of the restaurant opened to windows, and we feasted our eyes on a spectacular view of the redwoods. We didn't want to leave. Leisurely we sipped coffee, and Jack stated that although the drive was beautiful he had had enough of the challenging, mountainous road and would take the next exit back to the freeway. It didn't occur to us that we had traveled miles without seeing an exit sign, and we soon discovered there would be many more miles to go before we had relief from the twisted tour.

When we finally arrived in Santa Cruz and found our campground, the stress of the drive and the experience of 101 paid off. Redwoods surrounded our campsite. We tilted our heads skyward to see filtered daylight through the trees. The effect was a hush of cathedral silence that inspired us to whisper. We quickly plugged in and pulled out our camp chairs and plopped into them with coffee in hand. We looked into each other's eyes, hearing our thoughts without saying a word. This is what heaven must be like. We listened to the birds singing high in the treetops, the tap-tap-tapping of woodpeckers, and soaked up the serenity and the pine scent of the forest. Later I took a walk into the magical woods. The quiet turned up another notch as I padded along a path of pine needles and golden red leaves. Trees and their limbs had fallen without a sound countless years ago and lay wrapped in moss and vines that dressed their bark in deep shades of green and an occasional yellow leaf. The entire forest sparkled in golden sunlight that showered down through the towering timbers that stood reverently, reaching their arms to God.

I sat on an ancient log and listened to the peace. I knew I would never forget this moment, this place, and this trip.

My reminiscing had carried me to the entrance of the George Wallace Tunnel. I didn't have to worry about height and other restrictions because I had been this way before. Jack Incarnate just mumbled quietly. He wished he could bitch. My ironclad grip on the wheel brought me through the tunnel to the bright, glorious sunshine on the other side. I weaved my way through the traffic, past Mobile's city limits. I was mentally prepared for the Twin Spans and Lake Pontchartrain. I knew I could do this twenty-three-mile stretch. I had done it before. Jack Incarnate was unusually quiet. He's not asleep, is he? I dared a glance at his fabric fingers. His soft knuckles were knotted and white as they clutched the armrest. Jack Incarnate mumbled again," *Did you hear what I said, Judy? I said you never did listen to me.*" He was not going to drop the subject.

"*Allright. I remember, but I did listen. I dropped the class, didn't I? I am not going to live my life worrying and fretting. There's a little ditty, ' never trouble trouble, 'til trouble troubles you.'*" I chuckled as Jack Incarnate sputtered over my comment. He was truly uncomfortable with that philosophy. And with that, I drove on, knowing that long, long bridge was coming up.

Yes, there were times that I rebelled and refused to listen to Jack's domineering instructions. During our relationship, everything had to be done his way. The housecleaning was a sore spot. The vacuuming had to be done slowly and methodically. There could be no sweeper marks. Footprints on the carpet were unacceptable. It was his wish— no, rule—that after vacuuming in the living room, which we did not use anyway, we did not walk on the carpet. So everything stayed perfect. Dusting was done every day along with polishing the kitchen and bathroom fixtures. Our home could have been on the cover of *House Beautiful*. There was never a dirty dish left in the sink or a crumb on the floor. If a dining-room chair was moved it had to be placed back into the same carpet dent its leg had created. And of course no clothes could be left on a chair or the bed, but hung in the closet where they belonged. The bed was made immediately, almost before my feet hit the floor and my eyes opened. You did not sit on the edge of an already-made-up bed to get dressed. Sportster, who could be Jack's alter ego, tormented me, ruining the twenty-five-year tradition because he would spring up onto the perfectly made bed and pad across, leaving a sunken path. Then he would stretch out into a yogalike position to demonstrate how long a cat's body really is, exposing his furred belly for an expected rubbing. There was rarely a perfectly made bed anymore.

There were cat footprints in the carpet and twisty ties and rubber bands, Sportster's favorite toys, scattered across the living area and underfoot. And I knew Jack would have been manipulated into tolerating these infractions because Sportster would have wrapped my tough guy around his paw and laid down the cat rules, wiping out any unnecessary Jack rules that might interfere with what was now the Sportster Kingdom.

I laughed now in comic relief as I thought back at my anger and frustration at living with a perfectionist. Women envied my perfectly manicured home, always joking, "Do you loan your husband out?" And although I laughed along with them, they did not understand the rules and restrictions of living in "House Beautiful."

Jack never wanted me to do any kind of project because he feared I would make a mess or ruin something. When I did tackle a project, Jack was always home and supervised the entire job.

I remember a rare time he was going to be out of the house for several hours, leaving me alone. I decided I would wash the windows. A simple project, I thought. I hurriedly gathered the materials and started with the bedroom window. It did not occur to me to go outside and remove the screen and wash the outside pane. Instead I lifted the sliding window out of its track and set it on the carpeted floor in the bedroom to finish both sides. It sparkled when I finished and I proudly placed the windowpane back into its track. I didn't need Jack's supervision.

As I turned away from the window, my eyes fell to the carpeted floor where the window had sat while I had cleaned it. There, across the carpet, was a black smudge the length of the window. The aluminum frame had made its mark on the light beige carpet. I panicked and ran down the hall to the laundry room. Pulling open the cabinet door, I frantically surveyed the cleaning products. Pine Sol, no. Comet, no. Carpet shampoo, *yes!* Grabbing a rag, I hurried back to the bedroom, fell down on my knees, and fervently began spraying and scrubbing. The perfect thin black line now turned into a wide gray mark. This was working. What time was it?! I had an hour yet before he would come home. The Windex was right there. I tried that. It seemed to transform the mark to a lighter shade of gray. Oh dear, he would still see that! I scrubbed and scrubbed until there was no time left, as I heard his truck pull into the drive.

I quickly plopped into my recliner, picked up my book, and pretended to read. Jack headed down the hall to the bathroom. Silence. What seemed like long moments passed before he came back down the hall and asked what was for dinner. My stomach unknotted and did a happy dance. "Oh, I don't know. What do you want?" And the afternoon passed uneventfully. I was home free. It was a week or so later that he commented on the mark on the carpet, suggesting I might have something on my shoes. I checked innocently, "No. I don't. I don't know what that smudge is."

Another episode of rebellion was against Jack's rule of Do Not Put Food Down the Garbage Disposal. I never argued with him and followed his instructions, but always thought to myself, "What is the use of having the thing, if you can't use it?" That troublesome thought lived dormant in my brain until one day when Jack had to take his truck to be serviced, leaving me home alone, again.

I was making chili for dinner and had been soaking pinto beans overnight. After a quick kiss good-bye Jack left for his appointment and I headed for the kitchen.

After examining the beans, I decided there were too many for the chili, and that rebellious thought reared up: *"It would be easier to put those extra beans down the garbage disposal. Wouldn't it?"*

Well, lesson learned that day. Husband, right. Wife, wrong. The sink's drain became plugged up with beans. The half-ground-up beans filled the sink and floated in the water with black chunks of smelly drainpipe residue. *"But wait! Maybe he didn't have to know. I'd call the plumber, beg for emergency service, and get this problem cleared up and the 'Right-Wrong Marriage Scoreboard' would not read, "Husband: 1: Wife: 0."* Frantically I called the plumber, who must have taken pity on my desperate story, because they could come within the next hour. It was just a short twenty minutes when I heard the truck pull into the driveway. Whose truck was it, Jack's or the plumber's?

Rushing to the window, I peeked out. Sun City Plumbing appeared on the side of the van. I was home free! The plumber ambled into the kitchen while I tried to hurry him along. He examined the situation and then moseyed outside to find the cleanout. I could hear the clock ticking on the wall like a time clock at a football game. And then I swore I heard the loud "Buzzz!" as time ran out, but it was the sound of Jack's truck door slamming, because he had just pulled in and parked behind the plumber's van.

"What's going on?" Game over. What could I do but laugh, look cute, and stroke his manly ego. "You were right. I was wrong."

My rebelliousness almost always seemed to get me in trouble with my man. I watched *I Love Lucy* reruns only to understand that Jack and Desi Arnaz could have developed camaraderie over their mutual experiences.

"So I didn't always listen, but sometimes I did. And I've made it across the bridge once already, haven't I? With no help from you! You are never any help! Your complaining and criticism just makes me so nervous! You could at least give me a few crumbs of encouragement!" I can't believe it! I am screaming aloud at this cloth-made man, who seems to have a permanent smirk on his cotton face. Did I make his face to look like that? I reached over and slapped the back of his head. His sunglasses would have gone flying if I hadn't sewn them tightly to his head. I had dared to glance over when I struck him, only to notice that traffic was snarled and had come to a stop. The driver next to me was staring at me. Suddenly the driver's face lit up with the realization that Jack Incarnate was not real, and he burst into laughter. Still pumped with emotion, I smiled hesitantly, and then, realizing that I could still be driven to distraction by just a memory, I burst out laughing too.

Chapter Eleven

My problem was I was exhausted. I had been driving since daybreak and traveled over five hundred miles and although I was chasing the sun, it was growing dark. I was going to have to save the long, treacherous bridge for tomorrow. I began watching for signs and, as if by serendipity, I read the welcoming road sign, *Shepard State Park, next exit* near Biloxi, Mississippi. I took the next exit and turned right at the stop sign, as another sign pointed me with the promise of three miles on the left. I pulled into the park and approached the ranger's kiosk.

"Good afternoon." The ranger greeted me with a southern drawl and a smile.

"Hi there. I need a place for the night."

"Right. I can help you with that. I can put you at a spot right on the river."

"Great."

"Is it just the two of you?" I hesitated a minute and then realized he was looking at Jack

Incarnate. He then laughed and I realized he was joking. About that time Sportster awoke from his hidey-hole somewhere in the back and had jumped up on my lap.

Laughing in response, I said, "He doesn't have any papers," as I nodded toward Jack Incarnate, my hand absently petting Sportster's head.

"Well, then, I might just have to haul him in," the ranger responded, enjoying the banter. He handed me the registration form that I quickly filled in and handed back along with twenty-two dollars for the fee.

"You are a long way from home. Where you headed?"

"I just came from Cocoa, Florida, visiting friends for Thanksgiving. Now I'm headed home."

"Well, welcome to Mississippi, ma'am. Enjoy your stay with us. Here's a brochure with a map and history of the park. Just follow this road as it veers to the right and then take the second left to space twenty-two. It is a pull-through, so you won't have any problems. Check-out is at two."

"Thanks so much."

"And you keep that friend of yours in line, y'hear?" He was still chuckling as I pulled away.

"What a nice man," I thought as I drove slowly in search of my campsite. I counted off the campsites as I passed, eighteen, twenty, twenty-two. I pulled in and with a tired relieved sigh, I pressed down the parking brake and shut off the engine. The engine chugged twice with its own sighs and quieted to restful sleep. I heard a couple of soft pings and tings as the hot engine began its cooling

process. It was then I realized I had noticed those little sounds because I was just sitting there in the driver's seat, too tired to move.

It was almost dark, and the campground was getting ready for bed. I loved campgrounds. Although they all had different personalities, their occupants were similar, the travelers, the modern nomads who journeyed in myriad modes of transportation. Probably the oldest form was the travel trailer, just two wheels and a hitch, but could stretch as long as the "Long, Long Trailer" in the Desi Arnaz and Lucy movie; or they could just be tiny and cute like the old teardrop trailer, just large enough for a hot plate and for a person to lie down. But now there were toy haulers that were trailers made to carry not only the bed and the kitchen sink, but also the ATVs and motorcycles for the family's entertainment at a remote destination. And then there were the tent trailers that are half trailer and half tent. Moving on up the scale of RVs was the fifth wheel. It was a trailer with a fancy hitch that attached inside a truck bed, making it easy to tow. And finally there was the entire family of motor homes, the class B's, C's, and the A's, the diesel pushers, and the freightliners that range from twenty feet to forty-five feet long.

These temporary visitors with their extended families made their home for a weekend. Over ten people could trickle out of a large rig, then gather around the picnic table for food and family news while they created cherished memories with a majestic state or national park as a backdrop.

Other campground visitors were baby boomers or seasoned retirees enjoying a respite from an extended cross-country road trip. Some had given up what they call their "stick house" permanently and had joined the ranks called, "full-timers." Everyone had a story, ready to be told with a little prompting: "Where are you from?"

Evenings were spent in a circle of lawn chairs or by a campfire, getting to know fellow Americans: their jobs, their family incidents, as well as the places they were headed and the adventures they'd had. Sometimes the time was spent getting to know a European family, with their rented Cruise America motor home, who were exploring the United States and its shoot-'em-up, rebellious history.

Days were full of more chatter and the gleeful sounds of children, mixed with the cacophony of music, from Mexican, to country & western, to the 50s. But when the sun went down, it was as if a mute button were pushed and the quiet hush settled in with the nighttime dew. Sleep came fast and hard as the cool night air drifted into open windows, but only after children's snuggling and giggling into the wee hours.

Mornings in a campground were like no other mornings anywhere. At the break of dawn, before the campground awoke, the black hills were backlit against an ice-blue sky. As the morning sun climbed toward the new day, the darkness was sprayed with its golden rays and the hills faded into lush greens and golden browns. There was no sound but a single bird's revelry and the silent shuffle of a rabbit, both unheard by sleeping ears. At some point the mute button was turned off and life returned. Stirrings, scents of coffee brewing, and wafts of sizzling bacon and eggs converted the campground from a quiet, sleepy hotel into the rumbling, hungry sound of a full-menu family restaurant. Again, the gathering, the gabbing, and the gesturing, as breakfast and a new day began.

But right now there was an aroma of campfire in the damp river air. The campsites were private and wooded but I heard quiet conversations and soft music filtering through the silence. With a heavy sigh I gathered up the last of my energy, climbed out of the cab, and proceeded to plug in the electrical cord and hook up the water hose. I was not going to bother with the satellite dish. A simple dinner, hot shower, and a book were all I needed tonight. Inside I heated up a mug of water for instant coffee and watched Sportster as he stared out the screen door. I could read his little mind as he glanced at me, and then outside.

"Just a minute and we will sit out for a little bit." Of course that didn't satisfy him and he jumped gracefully onto the countertop to ensure he wouldn't be ignored. I swept him up, set him on the couch, and then prepared my coffee. I then carried him outside, grabbed his anchor and leash, and hooked him up. I pulled my chaise longue from the storage bin, grabbed my mug, and plopped down in complete exhaustion. I then remembered the brochure, dragged myself back up and out of the chair, and stepped back inside to retrieve it and my book. When I came back out moments later, there was a full moon as bright as a reading light coming over the horizon, and I now noticed the river that I had been too tired to notice before. It seemed to smolder with a mysterious, luminous emerald glow in the growing darkness. And then I heard it. The surreal sound was like music or a droning. It made the hairs on the back of my neck tingle. I felt uneasy and glanced at Sportster, who was staring intently at the drifting river. I rose slowly and walked to the river's edge. The sound, the music, whatever it was, grew nearer and louder until it seemed to come from underfoot. And if one can feel uneasy and, at the same time, be moved almost spiritually, I experienced just that, as I stood by the moody river's edge.

It was now complete darkness. I don't know how long I had stood there, mesmerized, by the river and its song, but it was time to call it a day, a long day. I gathered up Sportster, my mug, my book, my brochure, and climbed inside. Locking the door, pulling the shades, I felt safe and warm. I clicked on the water heater and then proceeded to check my freezer's selection for dinner. I picked chili and cornbread and placed the serving-sized bowl into the microwave. As the microwave hummed, I sat down and scanned the brochure.

The Pascagoula River or The Singing River, as it is called, is famous worldwide for the noise it makes, like a swarm of bees. The murmur of the music can be heard best in the evening. There are various scientific explanations for the phenomenon, but none have been proven. Many believe its cause is born from a tragic tale of Indian lore.

The Pascagoula River gets it name from a noble band of Native Americans who inhabited the area in the 1540's. Pascagoula means "bread eaters." These people are now extinct, having drowned themselves in the river. The Princess of a fierce tribe of Biloxi Indians fell in love with the Chief of the Pascagoula band. Although she was betrothed to the Biloxi Chief, she left her tribe to wed the Pascagoula Chief. The Biloxi people became ferociously enraged.

Rather than becoming enslaved by the brutal Biloxi, who believed they were "the first people," the decent, peace-loving Pascagoula clan joined hands and, chanting a death chant, waded into the deepening waters of the river. The chant was silenced only by their disappearance into the deep, swift flow of the river's undercurrent. Many believe the sound is the death song of the Pascagoula Indian tribe.

"Wow!" I thought, just as the microwave dinged, bringing me back from the 1540's and its heartbreaking legend. Do you think Sportster heard it too? Cats were supposed to have a sixth sense. Perhaps that was why the river entranced him, or could it just be because he had never seen a river before? Yeah, that was it.

I wished I had set up the satellite dish so there could be some distraction from the gloomy mood I was sinking into. Suddenly remembering the TV antenna, I jumped up and began cranking the handle to raise it, hoping to get a local channel.

I twisted the directional handle until the TV screen lit up with lovely, modern-day electronic noise, and a news station appeared. I already felt better. I settled into the couch with my warm bowl of chili and cornbread and listened to the weather forecast for Biloxi. Life was good again.

A hot shower completed the prescription for a lighter mood. I crawled into bed with Nora Roberts' latest novel and read until Sportster's purrs lulled me and my eyes drooped. The river's song filled my dreams.

I was at work. The customer was a man who knew Jack and me from A.A. when Jack was first getting sober. Jack had never liked or trusted him. The man was asking about getting his cat groomed but I knew he was really only trying to take advantage of my vulnerability as a recent widow. He kept asking personal questions, like "How are you holding up Judy?" and "Do you miss Jack?"

"Well, of course I do, you idiot," I said to myself.

"How about a hug before I go?" I cringed as his arms tried to encircle me and I moved away quickly. The coolness of my reaction embarrassed and angered him, but he brushed it off. His reaction frightened me.

"I'll call for an appointment for the cat." I watched him as he gathered his hurt pride and strode angrily out the door. I sighed with relief as I turned to go back to the grooming room.

And there, standing in front of me, was Jack. He stood almost like a guard, still and poised. He was wearing the same gray-checked flannel *shirt he always wore. I thought I had given it to the Goodwill along with all his other clothes...? He stood there looking at me. My heart leapt with joy. He said nothing, but his presence assured me and made me feet safe.*

I awoke well after sunrise as the warming sun's rays lit up last night's emerald green waters and transformed them into a lighter, sparkling, blue-green stream. Children were already wading at its banks, filling the new day with gleeful screams as they splashed each other with the chilly wetness. A dog was barking incessantly and true to form, the campground was filled with the aroma of breakfast. If anything at all, it was full of life. The sweet energy of youth, the excitement of exploring, and harmony of family. And I thought of my dream and my encounter with Jack. I knew that even in death, just as the river cradled those noble souls, Jack would watch over me.

Chapter Twelve

After making the bed and fixing a cup of coffee, I sat on the couch with the local news blaring on a snowy screen and studied a Louisiana map. The more I examined, the more encouraged I became. I realized that I didn't have to go back across that long bridge over Lake Ponchartrain. If I had studied the map before I would have discovered that I-12 bypasses the Lake and New Orleans and I never would have had to cross it in the first place.

"You never read the right things. You're always buried in one of you books when you should be reading something that matters." Did he ever shut up? I was reaching my limit with Jack Incarnate's comments. And I now had lost my chance to throw him into Lake Ponchatrain. But did I really want to execute him? I didn't think so.

I knew he felt both the fear and the love of the road's unknown end. He had been bickering with me from the passenger seat, silently but incessantly, the entire trip, reminding me that something can go wrong with my house on wheels: running out of gas, tires going flat, overheating, or oil leaking. I was compulsively checking the gauges, brakes, and hoses. And what if I was five hundred miles from home and the red check-engine light comes on, then what would I do? He would be very quiet and had nothing to say to that question.

He wringed his cloth hands and padded back and forth when I approached the towering cities with their speeding, weaving population, that rushed eighty miles an hour on eight lanes of concrete. And did he say anything encouraging as I ventured down long, lonely country roads without passing a living soul? No, nothing. And yet he protested just as vehemently those weighty treks across the long bridges spanning endless bodies of murky water, as he did crossing the dry empty deserts without a drop of life-giving moisture. His yammering words echoed inside my brain and knotted my stomach.

On future trips, I knew he would be terrified of looming white snow peaks with their narrow, twisting, up-and-down paths chipped out of the craggy mountainside. His needling, irritated warnings would cause me to have white-knuckled grips on the steering wheel, as he would complain that we should have taken another route and I would, once again, wonder why I brought him along.

And now as I looked back, even as he loudly had protested crossing that never-ending bridge, his beautiful cotton smile lit up when, once on the other side, the dripping cypress trees appeared, introducing a small southern community of plain folks who strolled along steamy sidewalks, picking their way from shop to shop, glad to share some time and a story with us.

And after the straining, gear-grinding climb to the mountaintop, he gave me a high five as he feasted his buggy eyes on the view of forever. And in the middle of that sleepless, darkest night, at the end of that lonely country road in Big Bend, I had awakened him by poking him in his polyester-filled ribs and we both got hopelessly lost in the dazzling starlight. That was why I brought him.

The mellow mood from last night's dream had evaporated and my discovery of the alternate route had erased the dread. I quickly dabbed on makeup and dressed. Turning off the TV, I reached up and cranked down the antenna and then quickly surveyed inside. With everything in order, I grabbed Sportster and stepped outside. The morning was moving along with the rhythmic movements of daybreak. I could hear the ripple of the river's heartbeat, not the drone of last night's somber song, and the chirping cadence of the birds as they soared over the water's edge, swooping to grab their breakfast of bugs that skimmed the surface. Life and nature was awake and thriving. Sportster lunged in my hands as I tried to attach his leash. He spied a blue jay jabbering news of a cat's arrival in its vicinity. I hurriedly detached the water hose, rolled it up and, after stowing it away, unplugged the electrical cord. I raised the step and then followed the leash to its end where Sportster lay, crouched in hunting mode, thinking he would have blue jay for breakfast. He made his own chirping sound in protest, as I scooped him up to stash him inside. He was quite irritated to have his important hunting project interrupted. I closed and locked the door and my eyes made one last sweep of the campsite.

I walked to the river's edge and stood on its vibrant veranda and studied the view. There was only full-bodied life and nature, no death chants of Indian legend left from the chilling night's darkness. I silently whispered farewell to the souls, past and present, of this place, turned, walked back to my rig, climbed inside, and headed for the interstate and home.

I had gone many miles yesterday and I wanted to cover as many today. Settling into the rhythm of travel once again, I realized I just wanted to be home. The ecstasy of my accomplishment and warmth of my visit were fading fast. I only wanted to rack up as many miles as I could. I was relieved that the twenty-three mile bridge could be avoided and as I glanced over at Jack Incarnate, he seemed relaxed and contented. He didn't know how close I had come to throwing his polyester remains into the drink, either into Lake Ponchartrain or the Pascougla River, when he couldn't keep his negative comments to himself. But then again, my irritation and resentments distracted me from the stress of the journey and I chuckled in their wake. So all was well now, and I welcomed his presence as the miles clicked by and hours ticked on.

There were so many sights and adventures I wished to visit as I passed through Mississippi and Louisiana. The Intercoastal Waterway traverses three thousand miles along the Atlantic and Gulf coasts. Some of its lengths consisted of natural inlets, salt-water rivers, and bays; others were man-made canals, and provided a navigable route without the hazards of travel on the open sea. I contemplated the task of following its entire stretch some day.

The Creole Nature Trail was an All-American Road near Lake Charles, Louisiana. It was considered a super special National Scenic Byway. "Above and beyond meeting the strict standards for becoming a National Scenic Byway, an All-American Road must be the best reason for the destination unto itself. The Creole Nature Trail meets the criteria through its unique, intrinsic combination of natural, cultural, historical, recreational, scenic and archaeological qualities." That was quite a write up and I would like to travel it.

I crossed the state line, entering Texas as the day waned on and the sun passed me on its journey to the west coast. I pulled into a rest stop just before Beaumont, Texas, to stretch my legs, pour a Pepsi, and fix snacks for the road. I parked in the truck area, squeezing between a big rig and a motor home. Jack Incarnate had his head bent over in sleep but Sportster was roused from his catnip dreams by the sudden silence of the engine. He stretched as he watched me climb out of the driver's seat and make my way to the tiny kitchen. Before I finished putting ice in my glass, he was perched next to the water faucet and waiting patiently for me to obey his silent command. *Turn the faucet on.* I recalled a customer once, sharing a story of her cat becoming dehydrated because she had returned to work after a long layoff and the cat refused to drink from his bowl of water in her absence. I didn't think I had ever observed Sportster drinking from his water bowl. I dutifully turned on the water and finished pouring my Pepsi. I dispensed a mixture of raisins and nuts that I had prepared the night before into a baggie and placed it on the console by the driver's seat. Sportster, having sated his thirst, now stared at the dribbling water, another of his favorite pastimes. I quickly turned off the flow, grabbed my drink, donned my cowboy hat, and stepped outside into the bright Texas sunshine.

Travelers and truckers were milling about. I wandered over to a covered picnic area with concrete tables and benches. A large display board under glass contained a map and points of interest of the area. Beaumont, Texas, boasted of it features to lure the tourists. Crocket Street enticed the visitor with its Dixie Entertainment District and the Dixie Hotel, a famous bordello that closed in 1961. Gator Country Adventure Park was an alligator theme park. What did that mean? A real mustsee. Beaumont offered airboat tours of the Blue Elbow Swamp and riverboat rides on the Neches River, also known as "the last wild river." And finally, Piney Woods was a paddle trail on Village Creek.

And so the list of places to revisit grew longer and longer, and I stored it for yet another day.

As I strolled back, I watched folks pass my rig, pointing and laughing with one another as they tittered about Jack Incarnate asleep in the passenger seat. Unlocking the door, I stepped up into the driver's seat and turned on the ignition. Faithfully the Wizard roared to my request and comforted me with its smooth idle. I slipped the gear into drive and eased out to the interstate. I had an hour or more of daylight left.

The setting sun was creating long shadows trailing from Houston's skyscrapers when I approached the city limits. I crept along with commuter traffic as the tired, citified Texans inched their way to the suburbs and home to a dinner of steak and pinto beans spiked with chili powder and hot sauce. Reaching the western outskirts of the city, I noticed a billboard for the Stephen Austin State Park and decided that would be a good stopover for the night. The park was fifty miles west of Houston, located in the small town of San Felipe. Once again a ranger greeted me at the campground's office with a smile for Jack Incarnate. I quickly filled out the paperwork, handed over the camp fee, and listened as he gave brief directions, tracing the route to the campsite on the campground map. I thanked him and eased away from the kiosk. Glancing at the map, I then looked up to check the campsite numbers when I saw an armadillo amble cross the road in front of me. Sportster, now awake and checking out our accommodations for the night, saw the armored creature at the same moment. His body became alert and tensed under his soft fur as he froze, with just the tip of his tail twitching quickly back and forth. The prehistoric creature moved slowly, not intimidated, and disappeared into the brush alongside the road. Sportster was in a panic now as he chirped with excitement, knowing that if he could just get out there, he'd have roasted armadillo for dinner.

I found my campsite and, stiff with travel, crawled out of the cab. Quickly I plugged in and pulled the step out, then unlocked and opened the door to Sportster, who stood anxiously waiting to go out into "the wild." I had no neighbors on either side. On a weekday, campgrounds are usually sparsely attended. A towering canopy of trees shadowed my campsite and a woodpecker high above filled the solitude with a rat- a -tat rhythmic beat. Hooking up Sportster to his leash threaded through the anchor, I carried him to a nice grassy spot full of bugs and other creepy crawlies. He got busy immediately, being in the wild, doing his wild thing.

The Brazos River flowed by fifty yards away and I hoped it was not home to any eerie legends. Inside, I put a cup of water in the microwave for instant coffee and then went outside to pull out my chair from the storage bin. Then back inside again, I doctored up my coffee, grabbed my novel and brochures, to return outside once more and plop into my chair. The brochures told of the history of San Felipe and the area. Stephen Austin, the "Father of Texas," brought the first 297 families to colonize Texas under a contract with the Mexican government. The Texas Rangers also originated here. No ominous folklore.

The sun was now sinking into the river, casting gold and red wavy ribbons onto the blackening waters. I could see the alabaster dragonflies and yellow fireflies shining in the dimness of dusk as they performed their ritual evening dance over the water. Another day was saying good-night while creatures of the night began to stir. A mosquito hummed in my ear. That's it. Time to go in. Setting my coffee and reading material inside, I turned around to gather up Sportster just in time to see a raccoon scurry over to a trash can. I swept up Sportster as he squirmed and protested that nature and his instincts are calling him to "go to the wild." "Tomorrow is another day, Sportster."

Chapter Thirteen

Inside, after performing the evening rituals—pulling shades, turning on the water heater, and nuking dinner—I ate in silence, thinking about home and going back to work. My manager, Ellen, along with Kelly and Sheri were competent and had held down the fort for the week before Thanksgiving. The week before a big holiday could be a monumental task, because everyone wanted their little sweethearts pretty for their families.

The grooming business was like no other. The common assumption that all you had to do to qualify for the job was to love animals was a gross misconception. Yes, you must love animals, but dealing with their owners is the real challenge, and can make you or break you. I particularly loved people, and *that* was a requirement.

I thought about some of my "favorite" customers, Mrs. Janes, with her little shitzu. I didn't know how old she was, but old enough to show up one morning for her dog's grooming appointment without her dog. "Oh, I forgot to bring Susie!" Shortly after that her son began driving her. Every time—yes every time—she had to explain that she did not get the full treatment the last time. And every time she went over every detail from the toes to the ears.

There was this customer with her Scottish terrier named Jake whose dog was borderline vicious and didn't like to be groomed. The customer, with her English accent, would go to great lengths in her grooming instructions, knowing how difficult her little guy (who weighed in at twenty-five pounds) was to groom. We would explain that we'd do the best we could, reminding her how aggressive Jake was. She would just smile and reply, "You gotta luv 'em, don't cha?"

Many customers had excuses for their dog's aggressive habits. "Oh, he doesn't bite"; "He's just afraid"; "He was abused"; "She's a rescue"; and "He thinks you're the vet." "Can't you put a muzzle on her?" was one of my favorites, especially when I couldn't even approach the dog. Sometimes it was fun to watch a coddling owner try to muzzle their dog. And sometimes the dog bit its owner, "Poochie!! Why did you do that to me?" Others just threw up their hands in exasperation, rarely embarrassment, 'I don't know why he's like that." But my favorite comment so far, was, "He's a really good dog, except for that one time when he bit our little girl. Otherwise he is a wonderful dog."

The customers that didn't believe in leashing their dog were always entertaining. "He doesn't like a leash"; "He chokes himself"; 'He's afraid of the leash. He runs when he sees it"; "I have to drag him"; and my favorite, "He'll stay right here with me, he won't run away," as the dog bolted out of the door and into the parking lot, causing the owner to spend the next thirty minutes coaxing Sasha to come back, or angrily screaming at Jasmine for making her late for her next appointment.

The dropping-off procedure rivaled with the scenes from a children's' daycare center. The two- and three-year-olds that accompanied their parents were so adorable. They did not understand that their folks were not giving the dog away. "He's just going to get a bath," the dad would say reassuringly as he tried to prevent a meltdown in the reception area.

But the adults with separation issues, who cried, were not so adorable as they were pathetic. They were those who insisted that their pet could not stand the parting, even for the hour, that the grooming procedure took. They insisted on staying with their little sweetheart during the entire process. Many groomers did not allow this because the dog could be difficult to groom as it constantly tried to get off the table and into Mommy or Daddy's lap. But my heart went out to some of these elderly customers because their pet was sometimes all they had after their spouse had passed away. The younger, just plain neurotic customers, I had less compassion for, but offered the "stay with" service anyway.

I also insisted that customers stay with their pet if the pet itself was elderly and had severe health issues. Sometimes a pet was so old and fragile that it really needed to be put down. The grooming process could be just plain torture but the customer would still insist on getting the animal groomed. Usually forcing the owner to watch what the poor thing had to go through was enough to convince them that it might be "time".

So this was the grooming world with quick lunches at my grooming table that didn't taste quite right unless I fished a hair or two out of my sandwich while incessant barking or howling echoed off the walls. I had been grooming so long I could probably do it in my sleep. I loved all aspects of it: the customers, the dogs and cats, and my employees. I was never bored.

My business now, in Sun City, was only a little over a year old. Most of my memories were from the twenty-five years in my Riverside shop that Jack had helped me build. Initially, when we moved to the Sun City area over thirteen years ago, as we drove around town performing errands, Jack would point to an empty store for lease and suggest what a nice grooming shop it would make. I always let the comments slide by because starting a second shop would require a major investment in time and money. But as the years passed, and the drive became longer as commuter traffic increased, I entertained the idea more seriously. One day my neighbor, frantic with worry, called me at work to tell me that Jack was coughing up blood, could hardly breathe, and that the paramedics were on their way. The forty-five minute drive to the Sun City hospital from Riverside seemed to take a lifetime.

After many tests, the heartrending diagnosis was made: lung cancer. After many more stressful months of chemo and radiation, the doctors claimed he was cancer-free. The six months of hell now transformed into heaven. We floated on wonderful, joyous hope. My wonderful friend, who I had lost on the day of diagnosis to fight the battle of his life, was now back by my side with a new lease on life. We sat in MacDonald's having lunch one day as we watched a banner being erected at the shopping center next door. "For Lease," it said. This shop, which was in the small downtown area of Sun City, was next to a veterinarian, and only a mile from our house.

We were both thinking the same thing as we munched on our fries. We wrote down the phone number, and the rest was history. I remembered not toiling over the decision at all. I just did it. Another defining moment, I guess. The time was right and now that we were flying high from Jack's recovery, the energy was available.

I worked seven days a week, between the two shops. Mornings I opened the shop in Sun City and sometimes sat twiddling my thumbs for hours, waiting for an appointment. Jack would come down at noon and I would leave for Riverside, where my employees had booked me with appointments for the afternoon. Many times I put in a twelve-hour day, not counting the drive home. Sundays were spent in Riverside working so I could be at the Sun City shop on Saturdays.

Jack sat at the Sun City shop the afternoons I worked in Riverside. He would answer the phone and talk to the potential customers that wandered in from the veterinarian next door. Many of their questions he couldn't answer, so he would call me and I would talk to them. But he did have his sales pitch for the people. He spun his tale of the little girl, ten-years-old, who started grooming in her parent's basement. They loved it.

In less than six months the Sun City shop was showing a profit and my longtime employee wanted to purchase the Riverside shop. It was six months since the diagnosis; I remembered because Jack was beginning to have difficulty breathing and the doctors prescribed oxygen. The odors from the colognes and shampoos I used at the shop bothered him tremendously, and he couldn't come to the shop anymore for any length of time. Escrow closed on the Riverside shop, and relief settled in as I realized I no longer had to keep the grueling schedule or make the long commute.

There are times when you remember every detail of a moment. It was only a month later, returning from a full day at work, that I joined Jack with a cup of coffee on the back patio. It had been one of those beautiful California days, and the evening breeze blew gently across the patio. I remembered being contented and thankful that my best friend was there to share my day. I started to tell him about a particular incident. The two Pomeranians that lived behind us, two doors down, were yapping incessantly like they always did. As I began my tale, I turned to look at him.

"I coughed up blood today," he announced. I didn't say anything. We looked into each other's eyes for what seemed an eternity. Suddenly there was silence in the entire world. No barking dogs, no jets droning overhead . . . nothing stirred, not even the breeze. "I'm not going back to the doctor. There is nothing more they can do."

"I know."

His condition worsened, and I was so grateful to have the shop so close to home. There were good days when he would putt around on his Harley and stop briefly at the shop to say "Hi." There were nights of agony when he struggled for air as he coughed up blood. He lasted one week after the one-year anniversary of the Sun City shop's grand opening. I believed he just wanted to hang around long enough to make sure I was going to make it, because he always asked, every day until the end, for a report of the shop's progress. I didn't think he would have left if he hadn't known I would be all right.

After my conversations with my employees, I learned they had made it through the Thanksgiving rush with flying colors while I was trekking across the country. I would be home for the Christmas rush, and was looking forward to the routine of work.

As I stretched out on the couch, listening to crickets and other creatures of the night, I began jotting down the ideas that I'd had that day.

I made a list of chores needing to be done at the house anda rough inventory of supplies for the shop, and jotted down new promotional ideas. I was a list-maker and a goal-setter. I always got excited when a year came to an end. I spent the month of December planning and plotting the future. I couldn't say I make New Year's resolutions, but I did set goals.

My eyes itched in tiredness and I realized that two hours had passed and I hadn't had my shower yet. Easing off the couch, I had to disturb Sportster, who had curled between my legs. I was soon showered, refreshed, tucked in bed, and unwound from the mountain of miles I'd traveled. Yes, Sportster, tomorrow was another day that would bring us closer to home. I had traveled 933 miles and five states from Cocoa, Florida, still 1,620 miles and three more states to home. When I arrived home I will have racked up over 5,200 miles and a total of seven states. That's a lot of miles. *That's a lot of wear and tear on the engine.* The mumbling came from the passenger seat. I had thought he had dozed off but he never slept, it seemed.

I lay awake for a long time, thinking of my new goals. I couldn't wait to see my sister, neighbors, and my employees. I wanted familiarity. I wanted the security of routine. I wanted the challenge of work and the satisfaction of it done well at the end of the day. Who knew what the future had in store? I knew that my life up to this point had been full of surprises and wonderment that I never could have envisioned. Even Jack's death held more intimacy that I ever could have imagined. I now knew that roses had thorns and that during the bitterest winter, *"far beneath the bitter snows lies the seed that, with the sun's love, in the spring, becomes the rose."* Snuggled beneath the pile of warms blankets, protected from the night's chill, I drifted off into a restful sleep and awoke to the new day's promise.

Chapter Fourteen

With eastern Texas's first light, I bounced out of bed and dressed quickly as water heated for instant coffee. In no time at all. everything was stowed away, unplugged, and unhooked. Sportster sensed my eagerness and decided to bypass his inspection of the campsite. He and Jack Incarnate waited patiently as the travel preparations concluded, and we began to ease quietly out of the campsite and back onto the road.

The monotonous miles slowly added up as the day dwindled on. I was forced to set the cruise control since my eagerness to get home caused my speed to creep higher and higher on the long tedious stretch across Texas. My mind's hopeful image of my homecoming did not match my heart's dread. Home was not going to be the same. I am alone now and my memories were off and running out of control. What if I got sick? What if there was a disaster?

I remembered the time I had suddenly become gravely ill, ending up in emergency surgery. That early morning at home, at the onset of my illness, I had told Jack, "It's just the flu," as I crawled to the bathroom to retch out my guts.

"You are too sick. This is not the flu,." he insisted. I tried to call my employees to tell them I was not coming in, and was physically too weak from pain to complete the job.

"Okay. Call the paramedics."

They arrived quickly and, with sirens screaming, rushed me to the hospital as Jack trailed behind in his truck. Jack kept a vigilant post by my side the entire time. They had given me something, and as I floated in and out of my pain, my eyes always opened to Jack's worried but steady stance at the foot of the gurney.

The surgery discovered that an ovarian cyst had ruptured, spreading the infection throughout my body. I was a sick puppy. If Jack went home during that entire week I was hospitalized, I didn't know. Every time I awoke, he was there. After several days of recovery, I became aware of the close call and I cried in relief as Jack held me in his arms.

Who was going to comfort me now if I got sick? Who was going to watch over me? The knowledge that my sister would always rush to my side was comforting, but I still felt alone.

I remembered another time I needed Jack desperately: that infamous day in history, 9/11. Like everyone else, I will never forget that day. Jack had the news on, as I got ready for work that morning. He called me into the living room when the first plane hit the tower. We thought, like everyone else, "pilot error." When the second plane hit, my stomach clenched into a knot that didn't go away for days. I had to drive to Riverside because I had a full day of appointments. Listening to the car radio all the way, I heard the desperate cries of the announcer screaming, "Oh, my God! The tower is collapsing!" just as I pulled up in front of my shop.

I was late and my employees and customers were waiting for me to unlock the doors, unaware of the crisis.

"Two planes have crashed into the World Trade Center in New York and one of the twin towers has collapsed. We're not opening today." I couldn't wait to go home. I was scared and near tears as I thought of all those people in the towers. And, like so many others, I just wanted to feel safe and be near a loved one. I put a note on the shop's door and headed home. We watched the news coverage in disbelief and fear all day. I couldn't stop crying, and that night, in the darkness, we held each other tightly. No words. Just the safety and comfort of each other's arms was all that would ease the horror.

I didn't want to leave Jack's side. The next day we shared with neighbors and even strangers who walked by, all united in the aftermath of the disaster. The entire country was in a shocked hush. There was not a plane in the sky. I cried for days and I still cry today when I relive the memories. But I remember most the comfort and safety I felt in

Jack's arms at night. I might not have slept at all if he had not been there. I realized that if I were going to die, I wanted him by my side.

It has been years since 9/11, and I pray to God that this country will never have to experience something of that magnitude again; but if so, I will have to live through it alone.

Home was not going to be the same but was nearing, regardless, as the miles added up and the day droned on, with interruptions only for gas and potty breaks. By late afternoon and still in Texas, I approached the city of Balmorhea, Texas, and a state park of the same name. I tiredly approached the campground's kiosk, paid my fees to the ranger, and headed for a campsite. The campground was neat and orderly, with picnic tables at each site. I found my site, eased stiffly out of the driver's seat, and plugged in the electrical. I had passed what appeared to be an adobe hotel, a swimming pool, and two wooden bathhouses within the park as I sought out my campsite. Later, after fixing a cup of coffee, I took a walk to the pool.

The pool was called San Solomon Spring because it was spring fed. A plaque explained, "the park had been built by the Conservation Corps in 1936 and that 22 to 28 million gallons of water flow through the pool each day. The artesian spring pool is 1¾ acres in size and twenty-five feet deep. It maintains a constant 76-degree temperature and supports a variety of aquatic life in its clear waters. The spring also feeds a desert wetland that is home to endangered species of fish, assorted invertebrates, and turtles. The pool has plenty of room for swimmers while offering a unique setting for scuba and skin diving." I would have loved to take a swim in the inviting clear waters but, tired and hungry, I headed back to my campsite. The setting sun cast a golden glow on the waters while it backlit the trees, transforming them into silhouettes.

Just wanting to eat dinner and unwind, I guiltily ignored Sportster's pleas to investigate. Once again I read the brochure that educated the visitor about the area's points of interest.

East of Marfa, Texas, are the Marfa Ghost Lights. These lights are allegedly paranormal lights, known as "ghost lights," usually seen near US Route 97. There are claims of the lights that date back as far as the nineteenth century. The reports describe brightly glowing basketball-sized spheres floating above the ground, or sometimes high in the air. Colors are usually described as white, yellow, orange, or red, but blue and green are sometimes reported. The balls are said to move laterally at low speeds, or sometimes to shoot rapidly in any direction. They often appear in pairs or groups, dividing into pairs or merging together, disappearing and reappearing, and sometimes moving in seemingly regular patterns. They can persist from a fraction of a second to several hours, in all seasons and any weather, seemingly uninfluenced by such factors.

I was glad I wasn't camped near Marfa. I'd had enough mystery at the Pacagoula River. But as I read on, "skeptics discount the paranormal sources for the lights, attributing them to ordinary lights, such as vehicle headlights, or ranch lights, or astronomical objects." Well, good. I was tempted to put the place on my "come back to" list.

I calculated my miles for the day: 658. Wow! But still in Texas. I made phone calls informing everyone that I predicted only two more days on the road. With well wishes received, I made a sandwich and stared out the window. Two more days. Two more days in my cocoon. Two more days of freedom from responsibility. The last of the constant motion, the continuous country music, and the unbroken ribbon of asphalt. The last of the breathtaking vistas, solemn historic sights, and the end of silent, starry nights. Maybe I was not that anxious to go home. As much as I wanted to go home, I didn't want to go home. *Are you crazy! I will never understand you, Judy! Women! They never know what they want.* Jack Incarnate shifted in his seat. I could tell he was getting restless too. What would become of him? I was sure he worried. As much as he'd fretted and fussed, I knew he wondered how long he would have to sit idly by, waiting for the next adventure. Would there be another adventure?

I finished my sandwich, changed into my pajamas, and crawled wearily into bed. Sportster perked up his little head from his spot on the couch and hurriedly padded into bed. With loud purrs he waited patiently as I raised the covers, allowing him to burrow deep into slumber-land. He was the only member of the entourage who never worried about tomorrow.

Chapter Fifteen

"*Six days on the road and I'm gonna make it home tonight...my hometown's comin' in sight, if you think I'm happy, you're right. Six days on the road and I'm gonna make it home tonight...*" Well, not tonight, but tomorrow night. Dave Dudley's classic song of a trucker on the road played in my head as, once again, at morning's first light I packed up, unhooked, and unplugged. The rushed travel preparations were becoming routine as I eagerly anticipated the next two days, anxious to take that last exit, that last turn, and pull into the familiarity and friendliness of my hometown. Jack Incarnate was tapping his fabric fingers to the beat in my head as once again the interstate stretched out in front of us, pointing the long way home.

Nothing stayed in my mind for long as I danced over each subject, reviewing my future plans. Excitement was overruling fear today, as I pictured the renovations to the house, the hubbub of my business projections, and the list of "come back to" places to visit.

The hope that life could be good, even alone, was stimulating. The days and details of this adventure scrolled across my memory: the faces with no names that lit up in rest stops when they met Jack Incarnate, the rangers whose day probably peaked when they encountered him and Sportster, and the campers whose friendliness filled the evening's emptiness with their words of encouragement and amazement at my endeavors—although I sometimes evoked unwanted emotions in the wives, who imagined someday they could be in my situation. Would they, could they, do what I was doing? I hoped they would remember me, if such misfortune ever visited their camp.

Sportster had been the best travel companion I could have ever wished for. He had developed his own routine in his travel world. The first facet of his routine began as a warm cozy-looking lump under the covers after the alarm went off. This phase was to entice me to live on cat time. The time to get up in cattime was when the sun's warming rays announced with golden glory that the day was to begin, not a minute sooner. And if it were a cloudy day, the rule was, you get up only when the warmth of rays soaked into your cave. Then you arose in slow stretching motions, moved from the bed to the "drinking faucet" to quench your morning thirst, and await a treat for being a wonderful cat.

This was all done while he oversaw my making of the bed. He then politely busied himself with his other morning chores while I dressed and made myself presentable for the outside world. Those chores included batting around the twisty-tie from the night before and sharpening his nonexistent claws on the couch. I then prepared my coffee to the crunching sounds of his eating his feline breakfast. This was all timed in precision with my chores, so that his demands for outdoor explorations and adventures in "the wild" could be met immediately with just a "look."

During the second phase of his routine, he brought me outside to observe his exercise ritual of rolling, reaching, arching, and twisting. When he finished, I was then excused as he hunted in "the wild" until it was time for his precise reports to me, in which he walked and talked around and between the chair legs and then waited patiently for me to untangle him. He then proceeded to the RV steps, demanding entry to use his private facilities. He was into being "green" and saving the environment, so he never used nature's litter box. Just when I got comfortable again in my lounge chair with reading material and coffee, he would be at the screen door pleading to come back out. The procedure would repeat itself, rolling, twisting, hunting, entanglement, and then back inside again for a mid morning snack. Naptime in cat time was ten o'clock people time. And naptime lasted all day long. I never had to worry about Sportster's lacking attention. His conscious hours were a few hours in the morning and several more in the evening.

The travel schedule fit perfectly into his schedule. By the end of nap-time I would have returned from my day's sightseeing or, if on the road, would be ready to set up camp, and the rest of his day could be completed without a hitch. The rest of his day pretty much matched the beginning of his day, except when the sun went down. Then he had to turn in and perform his domestic duties of being a loving and adoring companion, which he did quite well. I could not imagine traveling without the little guy, and I was sure he would not be content to stay home for long. The travel bug was in his blood, as it was mine.

I was so proud of my Wizard of Winnebago too. By the time I arrived home I would have put over five thousand miles on the odometer, and the Wizard was running as smoothly as it did on the day of departure. Jack had taught me that regular oil changes were the secret to the long life of an engine, and I had been religious about the task. I loved every inch of my woman-cave. I was now familiar with all the clicks and clacks of the mini-blinds, the *tink-tink* of the cups in the cupboard. One window whistled when the wind blew at a certain angle across the freeway. I knew the whoosh of the water heater pilot igniting when I pressed the switch and knew the droning sound of the generator.

When all the shades were drawn and the doors locked, I felt safe and warm from nature's elements and civilization's responsibilities. My Wizard of Winnebago, as I compared it to the Wizard of Oz, had given me the courage to go it alone, convinced my brain that nothing was impossible, and helped restore my broken heart as it nurtured me on my journey. At home the RV would wait patiently for the next journey like a steadfast steed, ready to carry me away from my everyday life into a world of freedom and discovery.

Jack Incarnate would keep watch as well, waiting to oversee the next odyssey. His cotton lips were dry and silent, knowing his job had been well done, but he was ready to ride again.

I had experienced so much. My heart and my mind were overloaded with emotions and images from my travels. From the first campground in Quartzite, Arizona, with its quaint monuments; to the tornado's terror in Lake Charles, Louisiana; to the simplicity and serenity of Vickie's driveway in Florida . . . they flooded through my body in waves, my eyes at first squeezed shut, then wide open and swimming in tears of amazement.

We had all traveled through my grief: Sportster, Jack Incarnate, the Wizard, and me, from the Pacific to the Atlantic, from dark, starlit nights to surreal dawns. I had felt cold loneliness to my core and nestled in Sportster's softness. I had doubted my self a thousand times as Jack Incarnate reminded me of the "what ifs" and "watch outs" on this trip, but my mind had flourished, gaining strength in the harsh winds of his unspoken words.

I was incredulous, astonished, and bewildered. How had I come so far? Much further than five thousand miles. The first weeks after Jack's passing,

I ached with sorrow when I closed my eyes at night, only to dream longing, mournful, fearful dreams. Morning's first light brought dread as I drug my heavy heart from the bed we'd shared. I had not known how I would go on. I remembered a quote from somewhere: "*Do your work—not just your work and no more—but a little more for lavishing's sake. And if you suffe—as you must—and if you doubt—as you must—do your work—put your heart into it and the sky will clear—then out of your very doubt and suffering will be found, The Supreme Joy Of Life.*"

I could not explain what had happened or when it had happened. But it was better. I knew I was going to make it, not just make it, but I was going to *soar!* My heart still hurt, my heart still trembled, but amid those tearful beats, a new rhythm emerged. The pulse fluttered still, but I could feel its force building within my chest. It was going to be all right.

Life had gone on, swept me up, sobbing, screaming, flailing against it, but somewhere on I-10 I learned to float, then swim, with the current. Where it had happened, I did not know. But it had happened. The future held promise and hope of a new life, a different life. I compared the future to the changing scenes past my windshield. I watched in awe of their splendor and then felt regret as they vanished in the rearview mirror. Then, just as magically as they had vanished, a new panorama, almost better than the last, burst into existence. And that was life, filled with awe, regrets, and magical surprises.

This next to the last day on the road filled me with a mixture of melancholy and anticipation as once more I chased the sun in its westward journey across the great blue sky. The day disappeared quickly. The air was crisp with fall, and Christmas was just around the corner. I tipped my cowboy hat to block the sun's laserlike rays as the golden globe neared the horizon, fighting to prolong its last performance of the day. It was time to stop for the night but I could still squeeze out another hour and a half, maybe even two hours, of daylight, so I pushed on. With ten hours on the road I was weary but wanted to make it to Quartzite, Arizona, so I could say I had come full circle. My first night would now become my last night. The beginning of the trip would then become the end. The little town of Quartzite would now hold beginnings and endings for me.

Wearily, I pulled into the campground. The sun had already set, not waiting for me. I parked in front of the office and saw light stream out as a door opened from a motor home parked across from the office, on a lot marked, "Campground Host.". I shut off the engine and climbed out as the plump figure of a woman ambled toward me. I smiled tiredly. "I just need a spot for tonight."

She smiled brightly. The shadows from the streetlight emphasized her kind face. "Sure. You just take any of the empty spaces and then check with me in the morning. Okay?"

"Great! I'm tired and I'm sure I'll sleep in. Thanks. See you in the morning."

"Sure enough." She turned and walked back to her motor home and I noticed her husband standing in the flood of the door's light as he observed our conversation. I climbed back in my rig, started the engine, and moved quietly to the first empty space. After backing in and shutting off the motor, I climbed out stiffly and awkwardly, plugged into the electric, and then climbed back inside. I wearily drew the curtains, yanked off my shoes, and pulled a Tupperware square from the now-limited squares in the freezer. A thought crossed my mind that I had planned my meals well. It was chili that I had grabbed so I also pulled out the bag of cornbread muffins. Just two muffins left. In no time the warm aroma of chili beans filled the Wizard's interior, and I collapsed on the couch with a TV tray and hungrily gobbled down my meal. I hurriedly rinsed out my bowl and heated up a mug of water for tea. The water heater rumbled while I slumped back on the couch and sipped my tea. As soon as the rumble stopped, signaling the water was hot, I crawled from the couch, stripped, and stepped into the tiny shower one last time. I stood under the hot water for many minutes, indulging in its luxury. The tiny bathroom was filled with steam that escaped when I opened the door, letting the cool air rush in. I quickly slipped into my pajamas and turned down the bed.

Jack Incarnate was already nodding in sleep, and Sportster wondered what had happened to the routine of watching TV. But, being the easygoing kind of cat he was, he quickly approved of the new plan and joined me under the covers. Wow! What a day. I was too tired to check the miles I had traveled today but I knew it was a lot! I had pushed on through Texas, New Mexico, and I could say Arizona too, because I was only ten miles from the California border. All I was sure of is that I had only two hundred and fifty miles left. That was absolutely nothing compared to what I had done. I didn't set the alarm, deciding to sleep in. When I did get up, I would dump my holding tanks and settle up with the campground host before heading out. Even with a late start in the morning I would arrive home in the afternoon in time to unload two weeks of travel, two weeks of adventure, and two weeks of healing.

My last night on the road. Tomorrow I would arrive home, the feeling bittersweet as I lay next to Sportster. This last night was cold as I snuggled next to his warm, vibrating body of fur. I wish I could freeze this frame, this moment of bliss, and live in it forever.

My entire body purred with the sense of accomplishment. My blood raced with excitement even as my brain welcomed the softness of sleep. It was not pride I felt, but humble appreciation of the ability to finish what still seemed an insurmountable task. Again, I marveled at what I had done.

The last night proved just as spectacular as all the others on this trip. The darkness enveloped me with feelings of security, while my aloneness only brought a myriad of memories of the folks I'd met along the way. I was not afraid and I was not lonely. Whatever was in store for me, I was ready. Morning would bring a new adventure, perhaps not as glamorous or exciting, but full of challenges that would engulf and fulfill me as I took them on. I felt an urgency that life was short and should not be wasted.

I tossed and turned, wrestling until sleep took over, sending me into a blissful dream. *I was running through a field of flowers toward an indistinct figure standing staunchly in the distance. The figure stood calmly and quietly as I frolicked through the bed of colors, picking blossoms and inhaling their sweet scents. The figure was distant enough to be indistinguishable but seemed to wait expectantly but patiently as he observed my antics. Although I could not see his face, I knew it had strong features and a kind, almost invisible smile. I didn't feel compelled to hurry, but I knew he was waiting for me.*

Daylight only dimmed the blackness of the horizon. The day had not yet begun. When my eyes popped open, the plan to sleep in vanished, as my excitement to get on the road again spurred my adrenalin. I jumped up in the dawn's darkness and dressed hurriedly. Today I would bring it all home. The last day and the first day. I would bring home all the treasures I had purchased and the ones that were not purchased but priceless. I was not the same grief-stricken widow who had left home . . . what was it, fifteen days ago?

The miles and time had stitched the ragged tears in my heart. The vistas and open spaces had wrapped me in healing warmth like a poultice, drawing out the poisoned depression. The hurt still burned like a glowing ember under the disguise of cooling ashes. The hot pockets of love and desire would not die out quickly, but they were ebbing.

Sportster stayed huddled in the covers as I moved them into place, quickly tugging and tucking them one last time. After a quick glance in the mirror and a "good enough" nod of approval to the image, I heated up a cup of instant coffee and surveyed the interior, waiting for the microwave's beep. My eyes were X-rays as I inventoried each cabinet's contents. All were stuffed and bulging with mementos, memories, and maps. The souvenirs of my trip. Still overwhelmed by my accomplishment, I distractedly raised the window shade. My already overstimulated senses were suddenly flooded to overflowing as they tried to absorb the desert morning's last gift to me.

The distant mountains burst into my living room. My eyes open wide with wonder at the illusion. It was as if, inside my RV, were snow-capped rugged peaks with a hawk circling in the foreground, its wingtip seemingly close enough to knock my coffee mug to the floor. This was what RV'ing was all about. People paid exorbitant sums of money building "stick houses" to have this majestic view in their living room. And me, I just paid thirty-two fifty for the privilege to watch a golden, bursting ball of orange and red fire light up the morning sky above the mountains' glacial glow. The gray dawn colors transformed into a spectacular symphony of blue, pink, and lavender musical streaks. My eyes locked on the silhouette of that magnificent hawk whose wings beat a rhythm to match my heartbeat, and in that moment, we both soared to freedom.

This was always my favorite time: early morning, before the world woke up, watching the early risers. The small birds sang their songs of eagerness for the new day. A coyote moved noiselessly through the campground after a night of hunting. She headed back to her pups hidden in the hills, where a deer grazed, unaware of her approaching mortal enemy. These were God's creatures, life moving on its own journey. And I was privileged to experience this all from the coziness of my warm Winnebago Wizard, as I inhale the coffee's aroma.

I sighed as I silently said good-bye, knowing that today I headed back to reality. The real world. There would be no spectacular scenes, no engrossing engine hums, no intriguing stories of travel, no campground camaraderie. But I knew there would be different challenges and I also knew I would meet them head-on, horn blowing. I would raise the shades to these new experiences just as I had during my past quest, and I would embrace the future, creating a new and different kind of voyage.

I sat for a long time sipping coffee and letting the sun heat the cold desert air. Sportster finally greeted the morning with a grogginess that caused him to slip clumsily off the bed's edge. He collected himself quickly in cat manner, raised his little chin, and then padded precisely to his dish of breakfast quibble. His embarrassment was evident only by a small twitch at the tip of his tail.

Jack Incarnate seemed to be lost in his own thoughts of home and the future. I knew he wondered where his place would be at home. Would he be needed? Was it over for him? What was he to do?

When I started noticing other campers outside as their pets guided them to their favorite "meeting" spots, I knew I should wrap up these last moments. Rising, I rinsed out my mug and surveyed the interior to make sure all was stowed away. I pulled out an unmarked, burnished-copper box from a hidden corner of the cabinet over the bed. It was unusually heavy for its size, and I used both hands to carry it over and set it in Jack Incarnate's lap, making sure it was set securely and would not tip. I then proceeded to grab my purse and head for the office to settle up my bill. Sportster watched from his perch on the dash while Jack Incarnate gazed forward, absorbed in the view and his memories of Quartzite. *How many times had we come here together? And my first marriage was here. We had bought that tea set for our new home from a vendor here. We shopped and shared meals with my granddaughter and great-grandchildren here. We slept under these Quartzite stars every January for the past five years or so. And we stood in the Hi Jolly cemetery as we pondered the souls who had eternally laid their heads there. We had talked about joining our ashes here in this hot desolate place where we knew quiet and serenity would be infinite under the desert's perpetual sunrises and sunsets.* A tear moistened his cotton face, unseen behind the dark sunglasses sewn securely to his fabric head.

When I returned I performed the unpleasant task of dumping my tanks one last time. The chore was routine by now, and I finished quickly. Unplugging the electrical, I climbed into the driver's seat. The glorious feeling upon waking was now subdued to sadness. I listened to Wizard's engine roar to life one last time, waiting for the cold clunking to turn to a warm hum as I routinely checked the gauges. Shifting into drive, I eased out of my space, hearing the truck's tires on the gravel road. My mood made me want to click my heels together, but I had one stop before I left this town with its history.

I drove only a block and turned right at the sign, "Hi Jolly Cemetery □."The crunching of the tires on the gravel was loud as I slowly pulled up to the cemetery's gate and parked. Now silence ensued. The wind was soft, only a breeze, but filled with the desert's heart, as it smelled of sage and sun. The cathedral quiet made me remember the time in the redwoods, now so long ago, so different with its lushness of life overpowering the muskiness of decay. This little, unknown spot of sand, was definitely the perfect place. I reached over to Jack Incarnate's lap and grabbed the can that sat heavily in his lap. Our eyes met for several long seconds that seemed eternal. I pulled my gaze away, hefting the box onto the crook of my arm, and climbed out of the Wizard of Winnebago. I moved quickly now toward the monument, prying the lid off the box as I walked. I looked up and around, scanning the area, soaking up every element of this moment. Noting there were no onlookers, I swiftly upended the box and marched reverently around the monument as the breeze with the sun and sage carried Jack's ashes gently to the desert's sandy floor. With the deed done, I walked one more time around the monument, my eyes to the ground. The ashes had vanished, mixed with the sand, and Jack, with his Cherokee roots, had now returned to the land.

Chapter Sixteen

The exit sign read, "McCall-1 mile." I turned right at the exit and passed the bridge. The everyday life moved through the streets as we all stopped at the traffic light. A golf cart slid noiselessly past me on the right and turned at the corner while I waited for the green light. The quietness, the sereneness, was probably only in my imagination because I could see fingers tapping the steering wheels, either to music or in impatience to get home to fix dinner. It was almost four p.m.

I knew this town. I knew these streets, the shops, and the people. If I turned left, the library and the post office would be a block down on the left. They'd torn down the old library and I wondered if the new one was completed yet. And at the next street corner was the local restaurant, the meeting place, for club meetings, birthday celebrations, after-church brunches, and half-price senior days.

The light changed, and traffic eased into slow motion. I felt I was dreaming and I did not want this moment to end. These last moments of my unbelievable odyssey. I pressed the accelerator, urging my Wizard of Winnebago onward. The last mile. To begin the first new mile. The last scene through my windshield transformed into the first look through new eyes. New Woman Walking, well driving.

Jack Incarnate seemed to twist in his seat, as if his jeans were too tight against his cotton waist. I could tell he was eager yet anxious. *Do you think the house is still standing?* Of course it was, but the question had always been brought to the table after a long road trip, just before we turned the last corner and the house came into view at the end of the street. Anyway, this was it, the end of an adventure of a lifetime that had consumed my mind and filled me with wonder. I was afraid now. Would mournful lonely thoughts flood like a tsunami into the now-empty recesses of my brain? What would I do now that I'm all alone? What would I do now with all of my time? I felt an urgency. I was compelled to live life, not waste a moment.

Sportster slept in what had become his favorite position, belly-up on the dash. His concern for the future would only be who had used his dish and litter box while he was away. When I observed his contentedness it always soothed me, and I felt my body relax a notch as I maneuvered the last turn.

There it stood. Home. It stood at the end of the two-block-long street. Jack Incarnate, relieved, slumped against the seat belt. Even Sportster raised his head, it seemed, almost in recognition of the street and familiar Sun City smells. I drove slowly as I noted my neighbors' homes that lined the street. Their rock yards were immaculate with their cars tucked away in garages. Not a car on the street. More than half the homes on either side of the street had American flags flying proudly and properly that would have floodlights shining on them in the growing darkness of evening. It would be after six, past the senior dinner hour and closer to their bedtime, with TV glows in windows by the time I would finish unloading and unpacking.

I pulled into the drive, pressing the remote for the garage door as I put the motor hom in park and shut off the engine. Sportster stood up, performing a long yoga stretch that erased five thousand miles; exhaled in a huge, teeth-filled yawn; and then sat down, staring at me expectantly. He knew he was Home. As the garage door rose slowly, I saw my car and golf cart waiting patiently, just as I had left them. Symbols of Home. I reached over, scooped Sportster off the dash, and set him in the crook of my arm while I opened the driver's door and climbed out. I made my way through the garage to the door that led through the laundry room and into the kitchen.

The kitchen table's surface was covered with two piles of mail, "junk" and "probably important," that my manager had sorted over the last two weeks. I made a mental note to go through the piles as I set Sportster down, whereupon he immediately headed back to the laundry room. He then spent his first thirty minutes of his "at home" time inspecting his food and water dishes and litter box in "his room" for any type of invasion that may have occurred during his long absence. Finally satisfied, he padded purposefully back through the kitchen, heading for the living room, when his attention locked onto his favorite catnip mouse. He quickly pounced upon the toy with the speed of a hawk sweeping down upon its prey and, with one faster-than-light swat, sent the toy flying down the hall. Then in a three-yard, three-second dash, he pounced again and at the same time, with one fluid Olympic twist, turned, and ran with pounding paws back to the living room. Moving with the velocity of a cheetah, he sailed gracefully over the couch, landing lightly, barely grazing the carpet, only to become airborne again. He then leaped over the recliner, ending with a solid, all-four-paws landing, as he stuck it, with a perfect score of ten. This performance was repeated four more times until at last he collapsed, his furry ribcage heaving in and out, as he lay, stretched out in heated exhaustion, with a whiskered smile on his face. He was Home.

When Sportster finished his performance, I walked slowly through the house, opening the windows and patio doors after removing the various lengths of PVC pipe from their tracks. The crisp December air rushed in to replace the stuffy, stale, two-week-old smell. Relieved, I found everything as I had left it. The rooms felt huge in comparison to the two weeks I'd spent in less than two hundred square feet. Although my home was moderate in size, with its fourteen hundred square feet,

I felt I now lived in a mansion. I stepped outside to the backyard to check on my drought-resistant plants. Although they were all healthy, I made another mental note to do some watering and sweep off the patios that had collected piles of colorful leaves in their corners. I made my way back to my motor home, stopping at the water turn-off in order to turn the water back on. Jack and I had made a habit of turning the water off to the house before a long trip, ever since friends of ours came home from a trip to a busted water pipe and a totally flooded home.

I opened the door and was pulling out the step when a neighbor's car slowed to a stop with a toot of the horn as the window glided open.

"Welcome back! Did you have a good time?" It was Ray and Geri from down the street.

"Yes, I sure did, but I am glad to be home."

"Everyone around here sure missed you." Geri's voice was loud, an octave higher than most people's, but at her age, it made her adorable. Ray, in the driver's seat, with his soft-spoken manner, smiled.

"Yeah, me too, I missed you guys."

"Well, we'll let you get back to work. We'll have to get together later and catch up. We want to hear all about your trip."

"Yes, we'll have to do that." The car moved on down the road as I waved good-bye. It was good to be Home. I stepped up into the motor home and stood surveying the interior. Where to start? There was going to be a lot of trips back and forth from here to the house. I started with the fridge.

There were only a half-dozen little Tupperware squares left in the freezer but lots of empties under the counter. I spent the next several hours sacking up food, souvenirs, clothes and shoes, computer and camera, up and down the motor home's steps, into the house, storing, stashing, and hanging until the Wizard of Winnebago was relieved of a hundred pounds and two weeks of living. Tomorrow I would vacuum and scrub floors, clean windows, and wash the exterior until it sparkled. Jack Incarnate wanted his clothes laundered to rid them of fifteen days of road dirt. But for now I unlocked and opened the side gate and climbed into the driver's seat. I backed out of the driveway and backed in to the side drive and through the gate. I eased slowly, very slowly, and slipped that baby snugly onto its cement slab alongside the house, with only a foot to spare from the roof's edge. The Wizard of Winnebago was Home.

As I climbed out, I glanced over to meet Jack Incarnate's eyes. He met mine in silence, but I could read the regret and sadness as I quickly turned away and climbed out, closing and locking the door behind me. He is only a doll, for God's sake. I swung the gate shut, secured the padlock, and headed back into the house.

I was tired. Weary and tired. Suddenly a hot shower in a huge shower stall sounded almost sinful. Perking up, I headed for my bathroom that was spacious enough to wave my arms around. I couldn't wait to stretch out in the tub, sink down to my nose in bubbles, and soak the five thousand miles out of my bones. Eagerly I stripped and did just that. It was an hour before I emerged, refreshed and relaxed, to find Sportster curled in front of the door waiting for my reappearance.

In my soft flannel pink pajamas with kitties all over, I padded down the hall into the kitchen, turning up the thermostat as I passed. With water on for tea, I sat at my huge kitchen table and sorted through the mail. I transferred the important pile to my large desk in my huge office, bagging the rest for trash just as the microwave dinged. After making my tea, I grabbed the magazines, moved to the living room, and plopped into my huge recliner, flipping the footrest up with a sigh of satisfaction. I was Home.

The evening passed uneventfully as I thumbed through the magazines. I clicked on my gigantic television and checked the DVR. My evenings would be full as I caught up with my favorite episodes. As twilight turned into nighttime, I noticed the shadows across the rock-landscaped backyard loomed, in contrast to dazzling bright moonlight. A full blue moon glowed over the entire universe as it refused to allow the deepening darkness to take control. My eyelids grew heavy. I was soothed by the large blue moon while I nestled in my huge chair in my large mansion.

Finally, clicking off the TV and setting the magazines aside, I pulled the lever on the recliner to lower my legs. Sportster, who had curled into his usual ball of fur with his tail's tip covering his eyes from the TV's glare, took the signal without complaint and jumped gracefully to the carpeted floor. Turning off lights and turning down the thermostat,

I headed for the bedroom, climbed into my huge queen-sized bed, and sank into the foam memory cushion as the down comforter stroked my cheek in a gentle caress. The plump pillows cushioned my head until I was completely submerged in softness and was immediately asleep.

I dreamt of Jack. *We sat side by side in the grass, our backs against a rough-hewn fence. It was so wonderful to see him. I was so excited. I told him desperately that I had thought that I would never see him again. We talked about little things and "how are yous.". He explained that they kept him busy where he was and he seemed contented and happy. I told him how much I desperately missed him. My heart ached even in sleep, during this wonderful dream. I told him that some people thought we had split up. There had been many who thought we would never last. I told him, "They don't understand why you are gone." He moved to stand up, explaining with regret that he had to go. I begged him not to go.*

"You can go with me," he said. In the dream, it was a decision that was possible to make.

Suddenly I was consumed in agony as I wrapped my arms tightly around him. "I can't!" Those two words brought wrenching sobs that shook me to the core. "I can't!" In the dream I knew I could only make that decision, that I had to let him go. He was understanding and all knowing, and I knew this was good-bye. I awoke, crying the mournful cry of a soul split in half.

Chapter Seventeen

It was late summer and late afternoon, before daylight savings changed time and robbed the day of those magical hours, just before nightfall. It had been seven months since my return from the Land of Oz. The evening's balmy breeze drifted across the patio and moved the swing slightly back and forth as I stretched out, surveying my surroundings.

The back patio had been completed several months ago. The ugly green carpeting had been ripped up and replaced by fresh beige carpet that blended with the house's aluminum siding. I'd had the side patio, formerly covered in peeling green paint, tiled to match the kitchen's muted brown ceramic floor. From inside the kitchen, the side patio could be viewed giving the impression that the kitchen flowed outside into either the dusk of evening or the warm glow of morning.

The barbeque was sending an aromatic, hunger-stirring haze of hamburger smoke billowing across my prone position. My attention to drifted back to my finger as it traced a route on the map I studied.

The potted plants rustled in the late afternoon air, their leaves swayed with the movement of the swing as I lounged listening to the soft country music strumming from inside. It set a mellow mood that all was good in the world. I had spent the entire day washing the car and the Wizard of Winnebago, spraying weeds, making windows sparkle, and cleaning the patio and its furniture. The plants still dripped from their drinks of fertilized watering, and I thought I could almost hear their squeaky, gleeful, thankful voices.

As I continued to lie on the swing, contentedness swept over me until my stomach reminded me of the burger on the barbeque. Rising, I laid the map aside, approached the grill, and lifted the lid as the sweet-smelling smoke swept up into my nose, watering my eyes. I had already prepared the fixin's, set the patio table with a napkin, and brought out a salad of cherry tomatoes and avocados I had tossed with ranch dressing. I quickly browned the hamburger bun to perfection and scooped the patty onto it. Sitting down at my patio table, I relished in my dinner preparations. While eating, my eyes scanned the paint job of the tables and chairs, another project of sweat, sanding, and painting I had conquered.

During these past months I had done so much: the new paint, the patios, and the back bedroom.

Although I had not conquered the wallpaper on the latter, the back bedroom was now redesigned as an art studio. My paintings covered the walls. I had joined a couple of art clubs, met other aspiring and accomplished artists, and participated in several shows. I had no success in the sales area but enjoyed the camaraderie of like-minded artists. It challenged me to try new mediums and subjects. I had experimented with portraits and completed one of my new heart throb and country star, Kenny Chesney, of which I was quite proud.

I was still enjoying dabbling in the art field, but my ambition had dimmed because I was realizing that promoting one's art was a hard and time-consuming job. The packing up of the art for a show, the unloading, the hours spent, sometimes in the hot sun, or in winds that threatened toppling over the displays, all while trying to work full time during the week, was becoming too burdensome, especially with no encouragement from sales. I was honest enough with myself to understand my art was good, but not that good. I decided to just persue it as an enjoyable hobby. I still took pleasure in sitting in the shade at my campsite, attempting to recreate a scene in oil or pastel of a past vista that had taken my breath away. The challenge was invigorating but the results were usually elusive.

After my return from my odyssey, the days and months had passed quickly and almost uneventfully until three months ago. I had left my grooming shop and was driving through the shopping center's parking lot, heading for the street. Suddenly, a loud metal *bang!*—I felt the car jolt like a seven-point quake. My foot slammed down on the brake and metal screeched on metal. To my right, a car had backed out of its spot and rammed into my passenger-side door. I jumped out, fully indignant, certain that the driver was a senior, too old to have the flexibility to turn his head to watch for traffic.

My car was not a new car but it was in perfect condition. Not a dent. Well, there was one small dent on the passenger door where someone had dinged it in a parking lot. You really had to look close to see it, but Jack had always wanted to have it fixed because he obsessed about perfection. I had told him I was not going to spend money on a dent that you could hardly see.

I moved around to the passenger's side. Not only was the entire door caved in, but also the rearview mirror was hanging by a wire. *Well, Jack, it looks like you got your way. The dent is going to be fixed now.* I pulled my eyes away from the carnage of my beloved car and looked up to find a woman in her thirties surveying the damage she had done.

"I'm so sorry! I'm so sorry!" Her fingers twisted together in a knot.

"What were you thinking?!"

"I'm so sorry," she repeated, not knowing what else to say.

There are two little men who had taken up residence in my head: one is quiet, sane, and laid back. The other is insane. The latter was screaming, while stomping his tiny feet, *Look at the car! Can you believe it! What was she thinking? Hit her!*

Stepping out from behind Crazy Carl, however, was Laid-Back Larry, in a smoking jacket and with a cigar between his stained fingers. He set down the book he'd been reading. *Here, here! What do we have here? She's waving her insurance card, so you have nothing to worry about. It's just the door, you can still drive the car.* A puff of smelly smoke curled around his face as he took a long lazy drag. I pulled my attention away from Crazy Carl and tightened my lips to a firm line.

"That's okay. We'll exchange insurance info and be on our way. I'm okay. Really." I was calmer now.

After the incident was over and the insurance company contacted, I worried the car would not be restored to its original perfection—well, minus the dent. I called Jack's old friend Blaine, who still checked on me regularly as he had promised Jack. Blaine, of course, knew about cars. And I knew he would see the repair handled to perfection, as he was a perfectionist too. When I took the car to the repair shop, I mentioned Blaine's name. From the back recesses of the building, where the important people were hidden came the owner himself who walked me through the process with kid gloves, reassuring me all would be done to perfection. I was then given a ride to the rental car company.

"We only have a Dodge truck or a Chrysler Sebring available, and both are $5.00 more a day than your insurance pays." Crazy Carl peeked his head around the corner but once again, Laid-Back Larry pulled him back and stepped up to the plate.

"Whatever." I had been very stressed about the entire incident and hated dealing with the responsibility. "I don't want a truck, so I'll take the Sebring."

"Great!" She had a cheerful smile and a perfect personality for dealing with customers who had just come from mishaps that disrupted their lives. "It's a convertible. Can I show you how it works?"

"No." I said grumpily. Her cheeriness was not rubbing off. "I don't care about that." Her perkiness faded only a notch as she finished up the paperwork and sent me on my way.

At home I pulled into the garage and pushed the remote to lower the door. Inside I went straight to my recliner, and sat down with a relieved sigh. I felt good about the repair shop, and now I had a car to drive even though it was costing me. I had decided I would take it back the next day after work and trade it for one the insurance covered. I sat there for a while, unwinding, and then I heard Crazy Carl whispering, *Why don't you check out the convertible, just see how the top goes down? Take it for a spin. You're taking it back tomorrow.*

I shifted my weight in the recliner. It was only one in the afternoon and it was a beautiful eighty-degree California day. I proceeded to the garage and pressed its remote. With a loud rumbling, the door slowly rose. The sun spilled into the dark garage and the car seemed to sparkle like pixie dust. I climbed into the passenger seat and opened the glove box compartment, retrieving the owner's manual. In less than ten minutes. I had the car backed out of the garage, and, with a push of a button, the top crept up over my head, moving back as it folded down and disappeared. Wow!

A scene of nostalgia burst into my memory. I was sixteen again. My girlfriend and I were in her new little red Buick she had gotten for her birthday, We had been cruising about town looking for Brad whom I'd had a heavy crush on all through high school. We wanted to stop at the "in spot," McDonald's, for lunch in hopes we would run into him there. French fries were ten cents. The procedure was to pull over somewhere, just before we arrived, and put the convertible top back up. Although it had been down while we cruised the town, we put it back up so when we pulled into McDonald's and parked, we drew everyone's attention while the convertible top slowly raised, moved over our heads, folded down, and disappeared. We were hot stuff in that car!

Although it was now forty years later, Crazy Carl urged me to disregard that minor fact. I went back into the house and called my girlfriend. I knew she loved cars.

"Hey! Would you like to go for a ride?" I described my car with the illusive pixie-dust paint job.

"Sure! I'm not doing anything. Let's go to lunch somewhere."

"I'll be right over." I hung up and with a quick afterthought I rushed out to the Wizard. Since our return Jack Incarnate spent his forced retirement in the motor home parked next to the house.

"Wake up, Jack Incarnate! We're going to go for a ride." I dragged him out of the cab and hauled him to the Sebring. I felt a little sadness emanating from the Wizard as it watched while I squished his polyester body into the corner of the backseat and secured him with the Sebring's seat belt. I ran back in, grabbed my purse, and in minutes was blatantly honking in front of my friend's house. She came running out, laughing loudly as she leapt into the passenger seat like a teenager.

"I see you brought Jack Incarnate along." She giggled.

"Yeah. He needed to get out. He's been cooped up for so long." I floored the accelerator before she finished buckling her seat belt, and the tires squealed.

"Wow! I didn't know you had it in you!"

"Well, it's a rental, and it's nice not to have to worry about tires and transmissions." Our hair was whipping in our faces when we approached the freeway on-ramp. "Let's go to the casino for lunch. They have valet parking. It will be fun with Jack Incarnate in the backseat." We *bellowed* in song to Waylon Jennings's, "Mommas Don't Let Your Babies Grow Up to Be Cowboys," Tears came to our eyes as I once again put the pedal to the metal, but not from the wind in our faces: the tears streamed down in hysterical laughter as we glanced to the backseat to watch Jack Incarnate, his head bopping back and forth, giving the illusion that he was rocking to the country beat when actually it was only the wind whipping his head.

With the Chrysler's tires squealing, we pulled up in front of the casino, weak with laughter. The valet tried his best to appear regal as he opened the car door.

"You keep an eye on our guy, will you? We don't want him wandering off!" We laughed again, uncontrollably, "Oh yeah, and he's a big tipper too!" We headed into the casino as the valet stared after us.

That had been a special day for my girlfriend and me. She mentioned it often, in our later conversations, that it was one of the best times she had in a long time. She died six months later. When I think of her I remember that day, and I am remeinded that good things came out of what seemed to be bad events.

I finished my dinner. The hamburger had proved to be messily juicy and the salad crisp and cold pulling my mind back to the present. The evening sky was bursting with California's usual blues and pinks as the sun took its exit from another day of accomplishment and satisfaction. Those fears I entertained months ago on the road, of what the future had in store, had been unfounded. There had been no major disasters or illnesses, only what I would call glitches, and those kept my life from being mundane. Of course, I knew I was not immune to disasters and illness, I thought as I cleared the table and carried my plate and utensils into the kitchen, but I now realized I could handle just about anything. I had made friends and solidified my relationship with my sister. I had not let time stand still as I completed old projects and busied myself with new ones. I worked with a fervor at everything I did, afraid if I stopped, I would remember—and even more afraid I wouldn't. I compared my cross-country odyssey to a butterfly's time in its cocoon. How many hours during that five-thousand-mile-trek had it taken to complete the healing and nurturing needed for me to unfold my still-moist wings and dry them in the new future I was now living? This future was quickly becoming my past as I neared the one-year anniversary of Jack's passing.

After cleaning up the dishes, I headed back to the patio swing where I'd laid the map I had been perusing. I was getting an itch to travel somewhere, not just to the local campgrounds—I had been doing that since I joined a singles RV group— but rather to far-off panoramic vistas were whispering in the breeze, enticing me to experience their IMAX adventures. The singles RV group was a great group, mostly women, who were independent and full of humorous stories. I looked forward to their monthly campouts and potlucks, but my work schedule and the other girls' finances kept me from hooking up with some of the members for more lengthy side trips. I was beginning to realize a lengthy trip, if it were going to happen, was going to be another solo one.

The breeze tickled the maps' pages. I sighed, just as the telephone rang.

"Hello is this Judy?" I didn't recognize the unfamiliar area code on the caller ID.

"Hi. This is Brad Jones. Do you remember me?" The satin, soft-spoken voice tickled my memory and caused my stomach to do a flip-flop. I sat up with a jolt. It was my high school sweetheart! It was wasn't it? No it wasn't...yes it was!

"Oh! Yes! How did you get my number? It has been so long! How did you find me?" The questions rushed out of my mouth like a train heading for a wreck. *God! Get a hold of yourself, girl!*

"The internet is wonderful thing."

"Oh." Silence. I'd crashed now. Now I had nothing to say.

His voice had a nervous lightness to it. "Well, the reason I was calling, since you asked," he chuckled, "was that Springfield High is having a reunion in September. I was wondering, are you going? I mean, would you like to go? I mean, had you planned on going?"

"No, I didn't know. I mean I didn't know about it. I don't know." Now I was stammering too. "When is it? September what?" I was trying to buy time. I had to get myself together. Was he asking me to the reunion? Or just to be on the reunion committee?

"September second. It's Labor Day weekend."

"Well..." Heat rushed up to my face, and I could feel beads of sweat forming on my forehead. "I don't know, but maybe. I've never gone to a reunion. It might be fun."

"Yeah, that's what I thought. We could hook up with Jim, remember him? And then Alice and Bob. Did you now they are still together?"

"No way!"

"Yeah. Anyway, it would be fun. And I could show you around town. Some of the places we hung out at are still here. The McDonald's is being considered as a historical building." He *was* asking me out!

"Really! Well, Brad, I have to think about it. I was thinking about a trip in my RV. Going to Illinois would be a nice road trip and a beautiful time of the year to go too."

"Okay." Was that disappointment I heard?

"I'll think on it and call you. I'll have to check my schedule. I am still grooming dogs, you know. I have my own business and sometimes it is hard to get away, but the more I think about it, the more excited I get."

"Great," he said, his voice more hopeful, "I hope to hear from you, and then maybe we can catch up too. It was nice talking to you."

"You too! Talk to you then." The dial tone hummed in my ear as I sat, slowly swinging but seeming to be frozen in place. *What just happened here?*

Chapter Eighteen

Brad Jones. My high school crush. He was my "bad boy." All the nice girls— me, being one of them— had secretly lusted for him.. He rode a Triumph motorcycle, smoked, drank (he was probably an alcoholic), and had the James Dean hair. He was all things a nice girl should *not* want, just like in the movie. I remembered how I had got involved with him.

I had been placed in a low track English class because of a bad grade the semester before and, of course, being the "bad boy", all his grades were D's and F's, so there we sat, bored to death in English class together.

Many times I would ditch an assembly finding them boring and hang out across the street in a little café where potential dropouts spent their time when they were ditching class. In that dark dingy café, Brad, who probably ditched regularly, locked lonely eyes with me, and we made a connection in our rebellion.

It was the 60's, a time of free love and my senior year. Eager to be an adult, I had convinced my parents I was mature enough to have my own place. I moved into one of the apartments they owned. There Brad and I had many midnight trysts. Brad, always careful in the bedroom to have a condom, and to remind me not to fall in love because he was a "bad boy." He would lay with me, sharing pillow talk into wee hours of the morning, his cigarette glowing in the dark, as he inhaled in relaxed satisfaction. In teenage innocence, I felt special in his presence, contented that, for the moment, he was mine and wanted me.

Scroll down past high school, from the 60's to the 80's. Shortly after Jack and I had married, my sister, Sandy, invited me to accompany her to our hometown for our favorite aunt and uncles' fiftieth wedding anniversary. Her husband couldn't make the trip, and Jack refused to fly, so it would be just the two of us—we would have a ball, she pled. We had not been home in over twenty years.

We traveled back in time. We visited our grade school and walked the halls of our high school. We sat on a bench, catching fireflies one evening at the pond in our local park, where we used to ice skate in the winter and fish for crawdads in the summer.

The town square was still the same, bringing back Christmas-card memories of bustling along snow-shoveled sidewalks lined with green-and-red-garlanded light posts, shopping for that special Christmas present for Mom or Dad. In our hotel at night we talked of old boyfriends.

"I wonder what they are doing ? Do they still live here? Why not just check the telephone book, look for their names?" My sister had always been more sentimental than I, and she reached for the hotel's phone book.

We had giggled like teenagers at a pajama party as we sat cross-legged on the hotel beds. Sandy's old boyfriend was listed, but she didn't have the guts to call him. Writing down his address, she shoved the paper in her purse.

"We'll drive by tomorrow. See where he lives. Your turn."

"Okay. Here goes!" God, I was nervous. I tried to calm down by telling myself, *But it's just a phone call, right?* "Hello, is this Brad Jones?"

"Yes. Who is this?"

"My name is Carrie, from Springfield High. Do you remember me?" A long, unbearable pause.

"Yeah, I remember you. How are you?" I explained about living in California, and just being in town for the anniversary party.

"Where are you staying?" he asked.

I gave the name of the hotel and we chatted about his work and my being married. He asked about my family and we shared small talk. We awkwardly ended the conversation with the usual "Nice hearing from you, we'll have to get together sometime," and he asked me to write, "sometime." I hung up the phone. My sister and I locked eyes for several seconds, then, flopping backward onto the bed, we exploded into bursts of laughter. I was giddy, and my sister was envious that I had gotten to talk to my boyfriend although she hadn't had the guts to call hers. We talked boy talk until all hours of the night. Who said you can't go home again?

The next morning we sat at breakfast in the hotel dining room. Our agenda that day was to find my sister's boyfriend's house and then attend the anniversary party, because the following morning we flew home. A man approached our table. I looked up and let out a gasp. The man smiled a smile that had always touched me softly in my loneliest places. I could never forget it. It was Brad. I must have stuttered and fidgeted, finally asking him to sit down. He looked good. Those narrow hips still supported bell-bottom jeans that hung low on his waist. His hair was still styled in the fifties fashion and those blue eyes! I honestly didn't remember what we talked about as I watched those full lips move in conversation, but I shared pictures of my family and basked in the glow of the past. Finally I explained that Sandy and I had to go, that we were flying out early in the morning. With nervous, *It was so nice to see you*s and *we'll keep in touch*es and *thanks for coming*s, we all rose from the dining room, Brad parting from us at the door. And it was over.

I floated on cloud nine for the rest of the day. I didn't need Southwest Airlines to get me home. Now I understood how people had affairs. My ego had been *sooo* stroked. But I was not the giddy teen anymore, and I would not break the bond that Jack and I had, even though we had difficulties, not for a quick lay in the hay. But oh, how I wished I were young and carefree again.

After a few errands, on to our next stop, my sister's old boyfriend's house, Dean's, house. We found the street on the map and Sandy decided that he might even be home for lunch, as it was past twelve. With Sandy driving the rental car, we pulled onto Dean's street. Reading off the street numbers, suddenly my sister shrieked. "Oh my God! There he is! He's coming out of his house!" She was screaming hysterically as she looked up and discovered we were on a dead-end street. Now she couldn't speed off into oblivion. "Oh God! He might see me! He'll see the out-of-state plates and somehow know it is me!" She was being a little over the top now, but it didn't matter because she had stuck her head under the front dash and demanded I steer the car. I reached over and grabbed the wheel, maneuvering the car to the side of the road as I watched Dean back out of his driveway and head down the street, out of sight.

"He's gone. You can come up now." Slowly Sandy uncurled herself from under the dash and sat back up in the driver,s seat. Once more we locked stares for several seconds and then exploded into laughter until tears filled our eyes.

On the flight home, "Are you going to tell?"

"I don't know. Are you?"

I still sat swinging in the swing. The dial tone buzzing in my hand finally penetrated my trance and I hit the END button. *Wow!* My heart raced while my mind danced around the conversation. *A road trip to Illinois. That would be a nice trip. Especially in September. The fall colors would be brilliant. And seeing Brad again, when I am unattached? How would that be?*

I didn't know how long I sat there, but the air became heavy with the chill of nightfall and I could no longer read the maps that lay strewn across my lap. Gathering maps and coffee, I headed inside. That night, punching and fluffing pillows until dawn, I wrestled with the possibilities of what the future held. By morning I only fooled myself, as to whether the decision had been made. By the third night of restless, tortured, worried, excited sleeplessness, I finally admitted the trip was on.

LOOK FOR JUDY HOWARD'S
NEW BOOK....................

Brad picked me up after school and drove me to my appointment. The doctor's office wasn't downtown but at the edge. It wasn't in an office building but its basement. After Brad parked the car I glanced over at him while I clutched my purse like a life preserver. Our eyes met. The kindness and understanding in Brad's gave me the courage to open the car's door and take the first step toward my future and the last step for the unknown life inside me struggling through its first month of survival. The irony of it all struck me even at seventeen. I could feel the entire world's pulse and nature's promise of life at this same moment as I was preparing to interfere with it. I swallowed hard; shoving the bile that rose in my throat as Brad gently took my elbow. We walked the walk to the doctor's dungeon.

As we descended the steps to the doctor's basement office a question screamed inside my head. How difficult is it going to be climbing these same steps an hour later? I was surprised by the speed and efficiency of the procedure once I had undressed and climbed onto the cold stainless steel table. The doctor was not what I expected as he talked in soothing tones explaining that he was giving me a bright future instead of taking something away. I heard his words but they did not penetrate the overbearing gloom that was enveloping me.

My condition disappeared as quickly as it had been created and, sucked into oblivion with surprising little discomfort. I had expected excruciating pain to punish my physique and alleviate my guilt and shame. It didn't happen. So when we climbed those stairs that led only the two of us back into the bright sunshine, the weighty load of emotions came with me and was almost too much to bear. Without Brad's strength I could never have scaled the steps that brought me to my now broken future.

Only an hour had passed when Brad dropped me back in front of the school so that my father could pick me up as usual, unaware of his daughter's new mark of maturity.

"I'll see you tomorrow, Judy." Brad enfolded me in his arms and what little bravado I'd bolstered myself with melted as I went limp in his embrace. I knew it was over. Would I see him anymore, like this? Would he be around to fend off the demons that would surely haunt me? And how could I ask for more from him? Although he had been my savior, did I mean anything to him? Were my feelings one sided? And it didn't matter anyway because I could not face him on any level. Yes, he had stepped up to my rescue, but I had not asked, could not have asked for his assistance, and certainly would not ask for more. Although I felt the fullness of what seemed like his love as I sank into his arms, it could have only been his kindness as a friend helping a friend. In ten seconds flat I had convinced myself that I deserved nothing more, the deed was done. I was on my

*own. We would again pass in the halls, sharing our
secret in silence.*

Follow Judy in her motorhome with Cowboy Jack, a life-sized doll who rides shotgun, and her cat, Sportster.   Judy and her entourage travel across country exploring vistas and venues. She is traveling back in time to her home town for a high school reunion. Confronted with her secrets, she makes a discovery that is totally unexpected and more frightening than she had ever could have imagined.

Made in the USA
Charleston, SC
27 July 2011